Workplace Conflict

Workplace Conflict

Mobilization and Solidarity in Argentina

Maurizio Atzeni

First published 2010 by
PALGRAVE MACMILLAN

Palgrave Macmillan in the UK is an imprint of Macmillan Publishers Limited, registered in England, company number 785998, of Houndmills, Basingstoke, Hampshire RG21 6XS.

Palgrave Macmillan in the US is a division of St Martin's Press LLC, 175 Fifth Avenue, New York, NY 10010.

Palgrave Macmillan is the global academic imprint of the above companies and has companies and representatives throughout the world.

Palgrave® and Macmillan® are registered trademarks in the United States, the United Kingdom, Europe and other countries.

ISBN: 978-0-230-58464-8 hardback

This book is printed on paper suitable for recycling and made from fully managed and sustained forest sources. Logging, pulping and manufacturing processes are expected to conform to the environmental regulations of the country of origin.

A catalogue record for this book is available from the British Library.

A catalog record for this book is available from the Library of Congress.

10 9 8 7 6 5 4 3 2 1
19 18 17 16 15 14 13 12 11 10

Printed and bound in Great Britain by
CPI Antony Rowe, Chippenham and Eastbourne

For my family

For workers' struggles: past, present and future

Contents

Tables and Figures

Tables

Figures

Abbreviations

AAA	Alianza Anticomunista Argentina/Argentine Anticommunist Alliance.
ACINDAR	Industria Argentina de Aceros/Argentine Steel Industry.
CGIL	Confederazione Generale Italiana del Lavoro/General Italian Confederation of Labour.
CGL	Confederazione Generale del Lavoro/General Confederation of Labour.
CGT	Confederación General del Trabajo/ General Confederation of Labour.
CGTA	Confederación General de los Trabajadores Argentinos/ General Confederation of Argentine Workers.
CORMEC	Córdoba Mecánica/ Córdoba Mechanical Workshops.
CPI	Conduttore di Processi Integrati/ Foreman.
CTA	Congreso de los Trabajadores Argentinos/ Congress of Argentine Workers.
ENTel	Empresa Nacional de Telecomunicaciones/National Company for Telecommunications.
FIAT	Fabbrica Italiana Automobili Torino/Italian Automotive Company Torino.
FIM	Federazione Italiana Metalmeccanici/Italian Federation of Metalworkers.
IKA	Industrias Kaiser Argentina/Kaiser Industries Argentina.
IMF	International Monetary Fund.
MTA	Movimiento de los Trabajadores Argentinos/ Movement of Argentine Workers.
REPO	Rappresentante dell'ufficio Personale/Representant of the Personnel Office.
SITRAC	Sindicato de Trabajadores de Cóncord/ Cóncord Workers Trade Union.
SITRAM	Sindicato de Trabajadores de Materfer/Materfer Workers Trade Union.

SITRAMF	Sindicato de Trabajadores Mecánicos de Ferreyra/ Trade Union of Ferreyra's Mechanical Workers.
SITRAP	Sindicato de Trabajadores de Perkins/ Perkins Workers Trade Union.
SMATA	Sindicato de Mecánicos y Afines del Transporte Automotor/Trade Union of Mechanics and Automotive Transport Workers.
UCR	Unión Cívica Radical/ Radical Civil Unión.
UIA	Unión Industrial Argentina/ Argentine Industrial Union.
UILM	Unione Italiana Lavoratori Metalmeccanici/Italian Union of Metalworkers.
UOM	Unión Obrera Metalúrgica/ Metalworkers' Trade Union.

Preface and Acknowledgements

This book is the result of a long personal journey into the world of work and the social sciences during the course of which, and through study and experience, I came to define more clearly my overall research approach and political stance. But the book is also the result of a long, although recent, period of history that started in 1996 and coincided with the mobilizations in the FIAT and Renault plants in Córdoba, on which this work is based. After six years during which workers' original collective passions and struggles became individual and distant memories of the events, the interviews collected as part of my doctoral research, between 2002 and 2003, helped to rediscover, through personal histories, forgotten cases of workers' opposition to labour flexibility and neo-liberalism at a turning point in Argentina's recent social history. However, Palgrave's decision to publish the book six years later made me re-write my original doctoral dissertation.

Over the course of the last eight years, between the start of my fieldwork and the finishing of the book, I have often thought, and doubted initially, about the relevance, timeliness and interest people can find in the micro analysis of the social processes conducing groups of workers to act collectively. Is solidarity or injustice more important? Are leaders pivotal in mobilizing people? Is collective action spontaneous or organized? What are the implications for theory? Moreover, how relevant were these issues for workers in industrialized countries? After a triumphant neo-liberalism and financial capitalism had defeated opposition and imposed their social peace, was it still relevant to write about workers' collective actions and collectivism in general?

These questions have followed me for a while but have quickly been superseded by new events, new knowledge and the experience gained through the research. The events of December 2001, when I was in Argentina and about to start my fieldwork, have clearly been a turning point. In December 2001, Argentina's economy collapsed and institutions imploded as a consequence of massive social mobilizations. Protests were violently repressed. The country, considered by the IMF until the very last moment as the best model in the implementation of neo-liberal policies, woke up after ten years of reforms impoverished and divided, but also rebellious. 'We were the first', would later argue FIAT's workers' elected leader commenting about the roadblocks used by the unemployed *piqueteros* in their struggles, a daily reality in Argentina during the second half of the 1990s and still continuing when I was interviewing him in 2002/2003. Historically, this was not completely true as the first workers' resistance to neo-liberal reforms could be traced back to the early 1990s privatization of public companies. But the idea of linking all these different manifestations of working-people resistance to a single dominating model was clear. Later on, the study of the past sixty years of Argentina's social history gave me more details to identify other typologies and socio-political contexts in which workers' mobilizations have differently, but relentlessly, appeared over the years. Silver's work on global labour unrest and studies in global labour history have further added to the idea of the transhistorical dimensions of workers' struggle, something that, if at all necessary, the new waves of mobilizations produced worldwide by the current economic crisis seem to confirm.

While the case of contemporary Argentina and of the history of its labour movement provided a constant source of evidence of different forms of workers' resistance and of their linkages with the broader socio-political context, studies on the nature of workplace conflict in the Marxist tradition of Industrial Relations provided the theoretical bedrock for the research. That within capitalism the employment relationship should be seen as a field of struggle in which an 'invisible frontier of control is defined and redefined in a continuous process of pressure and counter pressure, conflict and accommodation, overt and tacit struggle' (Hyman 1975, p. 26), became the natural companion to the historical and global recurrence of cases of workers' resistance.

Starting from within the Marxist tradition of Industrial Relations, John Kelly's mobilization theory has provided to my analysis a useful and articulated theoretical framework for the study of micro cases of mobilization and, particularly with its emphasis on injustice as the basis of mobilization, it has been a stepping stone for the formulation of my original research hypothesis. However, as it is often the case, theory and reality do not always speak the same language and once analysing the cases of FIAT and Renault, from the search for injustice solidarity instead emerged.

This empirical (re)discovery of solidarity moved my research another step forward in recent years, first by criticizing the use of injustice in Kelly's mobilization theory, second by further developing the theoretical anchorage of solidarity in the contradictions generated by the capitalist labour process and finally by attempting to summarize and elaborate these developments in a broader Marxist framework in order to identify what I have called in this book 'A Marxist perspective on workers' collective action'. Whether or not my reconstruction is convincing, coherent and supported by empirical evidence is for the reader to judge.

Apart from this, I think the book would have achieved its aim by getting workers, trade unionists and academics think about the potentiality of solidarity beyond its rhetorical use and of a way of looking at collective action, stressed at different stages through the pages of this book, as grassroot based expression of workers' power. This, that the possibilities for action are in working people's hands, should inform any militant approach to workers' organizing.

The book would have been very different without the encouragements, criticism, discussions, revisions and comments from colleagues. Thanks to Guglielmo Meardi and Ana Dinerstein who have supervised my work at Warwick and to Paul Edwards for commenting on my doctoral dissertation's draft chapters. Thanks to Ronaldo Munck and Simon Clarke for giving useful feedback and advice after my PhD's defence. Thanks to Anthony Ferner, Trevor Collins and Tim Claydon for commenting on articles based on my research while working at De Montfort University. Thanks to John Kelly for comments on previous articles' drafts and on this book's theoretical chapter and for his openness in receiving criticisms and in providing constructive encouragement. Thanks to Sheila Cohen for her inspiring work and commitment to workers' struggles and for her enthusiastic support for my writings. Thanks to Marek Korczynski who has followed the preparation of this book step by step and chapter by chapter providing useful editorial advice and substantial criticisms. Thanks to Manny Ness for reading and endorsing the book and for sharing his ideas and experience. Thanks to Pablo Ghigliani for his enduring friendship and the uncountable moments of discussions while doing fieldwork together, working on a common paper or commenting on draft chapters.

Thanks to Carlos Gallo for the cover picture and for facilitating contacts with workers involved in the mobilizations described. Last but not least, I cannot forget Pablo Fernández's hospitality while at Córdoba and his friendship throughout these years.

The book could not have been written without workers' active participations, the support of my partner and the love of my, now 'growing', family. The book it is thus dedicated to all of them.

MAURIZIO ATZENI
Loughborough, May 2010

1
An Introduction to Theoretical Approaches in the Study of Workers' Collective Action

The historical and theoretical importance of workers' struggles

This book contributes to the debate over the nature of collective action and the dynamics of workplace conflict by presenting the history of a cycle of workers' resistance, set in Argentina. The forms, time, sequence and outcomes of cases of conflict are highly influenced by different factors, related to the socio-political context and to the organizational power of the actors involved. Notwithstanding these contingencies, studies of workplace resistance can go beyond the detailed description of the specific case once it is placed within a broader framework.

Here Silver's (2003) comparative historical analysis of world labour unrest has helped to locate workers' struggles in a transhistorical dimension and to show the interconnections existing between the historical development of the capitalist mode of production and workers' resistance to it. Whether following the Polanyian pendulum swing of social resistance or the Marxian view of workplace-based resistance, the capitalist drive for profitability is time and again put under pressure by workers' struggles, forcing employers to devise new strategies to reduce costs and maintain profitability. In this attempt, four dynamics can be identified: spatial, technological/organizational, product and financial. The first involves the relocation of production activities to countries and regions with low

1

labour costs. The second points to the transformation of the work process by the introduction of new technology. The third considers the possibility for capital to invest in new industrial sectors and, the fourth, that of shifting altogether from industrial production to financial speculation.

Silver's reconstruction of the dynamics of worldwide labour resistance is important in many ways for workplace studies like the one presented in this book. First of all it is a reminder that labour movement action is crucial not just to defend and improve the conditions of specific groups of subaltern workers but also to generate, through example, social change and the progressive emancipation of societies. Second, the fact that labour unrest is a constant within the history of the capitalist system of production and a source for its perpetual innovation is a guarantee against pessimist discourses that dominate in the mainstream IR/HRM of the Global North about the demise of collective action and workers' self-organizing. As Silver rightly put it:

> ... revolutions in the organisation of production and social relations may disorganise some elements of the working class, even turning some into 'endangered species' – as the transformations associated with contemporary globalization have doubtless done. But new agencies and sites of conflict emerge along with new demands and forms of struggle, reflecting the shifting terrain on which labor-capital relations develop (Silver 2003, p. 19).

Third, the use of the four dynamics mentioned above as a framework for analysis, helps to establish connections between factors that have a real transnational dimension and thus to look at workers' mobilizations in a more comparative perspective, which is less dependent on national and/or contextual explanations.

In this sense the context in which the cases of mobilization presented in this book are located is paradigmatic of the pattern of capitalist development in the global era, being based on two of the dynamics indicated by Silver: the geographical relocation of transnational capital and the change to new working practices. The 1990s saw in Argentina, as in many developing countries dependent on credit from international financial institutions, the large-scale introduction of neo-liberal economic policies. These included workers being made redundant as a result of the privatization of public companies, fiscal incentives for transnational capital investment and, most importantly, reforms of the labour law system directed at legitimizing flexibility in both the workplace and the labour market and curbing workers' organizations' financial and bargaining power. Workers have reacted to this situation by defending their rights and salaries and trying to avoid turning into an 'endangered species'. The responses have been different depending on the bargaining position of each group of workers. Groups of jobless workers became the driving force of the movement of the unemployed, using the roadblock as a weapon of struggle (Dinerstein 2001b); workers in the formal sector of the economy used the workplace as a site of conflict, with trade union- or grassroots-led actions (Atzeni and Ghigliani 2007b).

A second important contribution to assessing the theoretical importance of workers' resistance within capitalism comes from the Marxist tradition of Industrial Relations (IR) and from the work of Hyman (1971; 1975; 1984; 1989; 2006) in particular. Crucial to understanding why workers periodically contest the set of rules and conditions that regulate their employment is a consideration of the role of workers within capitalism and of the power relations existing within this system.

Contrary to ideas of social stratification and a tendency to class homogenization, a profound class division exists in capitalist societies, not just in terms of access to consumer goods but also in terms of the power position that the possession of material wealth brings. Thus, if inequality of wealth pervades the system, inequality of opportunities will reproduce the same unbalanced society, in which the interests of those who depend on a salary to live will always be at odds with the business imperative for profit.

While inequality and the class divide are important to frame the social environment of workers' resistance, the fact that labour is treated as a commodity produces conflicts over income distribution and job security. As to the first aspect, 'the wages and conditions which the worker naturally seeks as a means to a decent life are a cost to the employer, cutting into his profits, and he will equally naturally resist pressure for improvements'. As regards job security, 'because the employer must regard labour as a cost to be minimised, it is in his interest to retain a worker in employment only while it is profitable to do so. This means that workers' jobs are always at the mercy of economic and technological vagaries' (Hyman 1975, pp. 19–20).

There is, thus, a permanent asymmetry in the labour-capital exchange relation. While 'free wage labourers' depend on the job and are often constrained to sell their labour under externally imposed conditions, employers are often free to choose the workers they want and to establish the conditions of work. Most important is the fictitious nature of the labour as a commodity – the fact that the employer is buying the ability to work, not work in itself, implies his right to exert control over the labour process and the working day in order to maximize workers' efforts. 'The time during which the worker works is the time during which the capitalist consumes the labour power he has bought from him. If the worker consumes his disposable time for himself, he robs the capitalist' (Marx 1976, p. 342).

The exercise of managerial control, depending as it does on profitability rather than on humanity, might in itself be perceived as authoritarian and coercive, and thus be a potential source of conflict. But once this is combined with workers' parallel loss of control and autonomy in the labour process, and separation from the fruits of their work, then alienation, too, contributes to increasing the potential for conflict. Work, instead of being a purposeful conscious activity that the worker 'enjoys as the free play of his own physical and mental powers' (Marx 1976, p. 284), transforms itself into an unpleasant, exhausting and dehumanizing activity.

Once we consider the number of potential areas in which the interests of workers and employers differ, it should not come as a surprise to see the employment relationship as a field of struggle in which an 'invisible frontier of control is defined and redefined in a continuous process of pressure and counter pressure, conflict and accommodation, overt and tacit struggle' (Hyman 1975, p. 26).

The idea of a basic opposition is also shared by a materialist perspective that, trying to overcome Marxists' paradigms, sustains the view that 'capitalism is exploitative in that surplus value is generated under the constraints of the accumulation process' (Edwards 1986, p. 321) and thus that 'structured antagonism', a notion that avoids the view that capitalists and workers are always opposing classes supporting totally different interests, is the term that 'refers to the basic split between capital and labour' (Edwards 1986, p. 55). It cannot be denied that conflict is not always open, that workers and managers often find forms of coexistence and mutual adaptation and that their concrete aims can also overlap. Moreover, even from a statistical point of view, conflict is not something that happens daily, and nor is exploitation, intended as surplus value extraction, a self-evident concept for worker.

Thus, the existence of a structured antagonism or of a conflict of interests between labour and capital makes workers' resistance a rational action, although it remains just a potentiality. Its transhistoricity, however, should lead us to consider the different forms in which it appears, the degree of strength and collective organization required and the institutional and ideological limits imposed on it.

Forms of collective actions: spontaneous or organized?

Strikes have often been considered as almost synonymous with collective action, and this is certainly with good reason as strikes undoubtedly represent the most evident sign of the strength and power exerted by workers in defence of their rights. The actual use of, or, more often, the threat to use, the strike weapon is almost a necessary condition for the existence of trade unions. Strikes, in disrupting production, do not just produce direct harm to the employer, but often also to other members of society. Hence, the idea that strikes represent anti-social behaviour and should be repressed has often found space in political debate and legislative systems. Thus strikes operate at two levels. On the one hand, they are the most evident sign of workers' lack of satisfaction with their salaries and working conditions, and are part of the power struggle at the frontier of control. On the other, because societies depend on workers' willingness to work, strikes have often also been used both symbolically to represent opposing class interests in societies and strategically as a key to social revolution (as with Rosa Luxemburg's mass strike thesis). Moreover, because of their importance for both workplace relations and politics, strikes have been documented and registered by statistical analysis and thus have been the object of measurement and longitudinal studies (see for instance Franzosi 1995; Kelly 1998; Van der Velden et al. 2007).

Compared to other forms of collective action like collective sabotage, working to rule or boycotts, strikes are normally more costly, and involve complex issues of group collective identity and respect for formal rules and procedures. Because of this, strikes normally require a consistent level of organization and, as an implicit corollary of this, the existence of formal representative trade unions. The logical association and sequence – industrial conflict, strikes, trade unions – may certainly represent an important pattern in the construction of collective action, but it applies mainly to workers in the formal sector in countries with an established system of industrial relations where conflict and trade unions have been institutionalized to a very high degree. The use of this model, which we can call 'institutionalized collective action', is, however, unsatisfactory; first, because it leaves outside the focus of analysis the majority of workers in the world who are employed in the informal sector of the economy where association by workers is difficult or forbidden; second, because it does not take into account unofficial walkouts in sectors where workers are formally represented, and third, by focusing on trade unions as organizers of collective action, it misses out the theoretical importance of workers' own capacity for mobilization.

In the third edition of his famous book *Strikes*, Richard Hyman rightly pointed to the fact that the untold story is 'that the typical British strike is both unofficial and unconstitutional' and this is because 'workers are unlikely to feel a moral obligation to a procedure which they consider discriminatory or obsolete... workers' consent ought not to be taken for granted, by managers or trade union officers' and thus that 'A more fundamental reason for unconstitutional stoppages is inherent in the employment relationship itself' (Hyman 1984, pp. 39–40).

The relevance of these forms of collective action in which workers' mobilising power is initially expressed in a spontaneous and uncoordinated manner is both historical and theoretical. Cyclically but relentlessly, grassroots movements and spontaneous workers' protests have appeared in many countries and at different times. From the Russian revolutionary soviets to the *consigli di fabbrica* in Italy during the so-called Biennio Rosso 1919–21, from the Resistencia Peronista (1955–57) to the Marxist-oriented *clasista* rank and file struggles in the 1970s in Argentina, from the Pilkington's strike in 1970 to the recent workers' walk-out in the UK refineries construction sector, from Caterpillar's workers in France kidnapping their managers to the reappearance of factory occupations and sit-ins in Argentina, Italy and the UK, workers' collective action has often followed patterns different from 'institutionalized collective action'.

Moreover, the frontier between spontaneity and organization is not always clear. An action born extemporaneously among a group of workers needs to reach a minimum level of organization if it aims to be sustained over a certain length of time. By contrast, a planned action can spontaneously take a different direction in the course of the struggle. Specific workplace dynamics, different conditions of the labour process and workers' more or less favourable positions in the economic system may all be factors that contribute further to the determination of the type of collective action available to workers.

The recurrent historical appearance of cases of spontaneous, grassroots-based mobilization and the different forms in which collective action, following the shifting terrain of the labour-capital relation, takes place are important in two ways. On the one hand, they clearly indicate that a solid basis for the theoretical understanding of collective action lies in emphasizing the structural conditions that generate it. On the other, there is a long-standing need to envisage and develop those workers' representative organizations that can build on this system-generated resistance.

While this book will contribute to the theoretical aspects of collective action and will aim with this to foster a militant approach to workers' organizing themselves, it will not be in the direct scope of this work to participate in the wider debate about strategies for renewal or revitalization of the labour movement. However, as regards the historical role of trade unions as organizers of the working class and as political actors, and the resilience and adaptability of this form of association to changes in production and societies, theoretical discussions about workers' collective action are necessarily associated with different approaches to the issue of trade unionism. In the next section I will thus reconsider some of these approaches, particularly, by looking at the pendulum swings of trade unions between institutionalisation and workers' emancipation.

The function of trade unionism and collective action

Trade unions are profoundly contradictory and complex organizations whose nature and function are highly debated. On the one hand, they have historically been the channel through which workers' grievances find expression, thus representing and defending workers' interests at workplace and political levels. On the other, because this defence has always implied negotiations over the price of labour, trade unions are necessarily invested with an intermediary role in the labour-capital relationship.

Revolutionary Marxists' views of trade unions have often focused on the contradictions generated by this intermediary role, moving from pessimism to optimism, depending on the different historical time and context, seeing trade unions' function either as inexorably limited to negotiations over the price of labour or as central to organizing workers' resistance (Hyman 1971). From Lenin's thesis of the limits of trade unions economic struggles in generating a revolutionary consciousness to Trotsky's attack on bureaucratic leaderships, from Luxemburg's emphasis on rank and file militancy and the spontaneity of struggle vis-à-vis the centralization of trade unions to Gramsci's critique of trade unions as capitalist institutions, what all these revolutionary Marxists' views evidence is probably the tension and duality existing in the nature of trade unions: an expression of both working class power and the search for compromise.

Among the revolutionary Marxists, Gramsci's (1969) analysis of the complex nature of trade unionism is probably the most comprehensive, not just because it establishes direct links between structural and ideological determinations but also because it envisages in the factory council an alternative working class organization. Starting from the consideration that trade unions, as organizations whose main aim is to negotiate the price of labour, are imbued with capitalist ideology, he then explains the conservatism and bureaucracy dominant in them as a function of the structural conditions belonging to their daily operation, rather than just depending on the material benefits of specific individuals. From this perspective, employers' recognition of trade unions as bargaining agents, involving elements of trust and respect for agreement, created the conditions for imposing discipline on the workforce and thus for reducing the room for democratic participation. Further evidence of this top-down decision-making tendency was also to be found in the increased specialized role required for negotiating at the collective bargaining table. Overall, in Gramsci's view, by accepting the role of negotiating over the price of labour, trade unions were also accepting the imposition of a system of rules created in a way functional to bourgeois ideology. In this sense, 'the structure of a trade union embodied certain ideas about democracy, authority and bureaucracy; the machinery of collective bargaining embodied the idea of two sides who regularly met to exchange bids and demands, and who normally reached an agreement' (Kelly 1988, p. 64).

Thus the logic of the employment relation as a market exchange between parts, with the trade unions' acceptance of the bargaining system, is not just ideologically reinforced but, more concretely, imposed by binding workers to a respect for rules and discipline.

Gramsci's emphasis on the factory councils as alternative workers' organizations may be criticised for not considering the extent to which institutionalization can penetrate even these class-oriented organizations (Kelly 1988, p. 67). However two aspects here interest us: Gramsci's vision of the factory councils as workplace-based organizations that transcend skill and sector divisions to include representation from the whole workforce and the need to contest capitalists' control of the labour process.

The first aspect, talking of a class-based, horizontal, open and democratic organization, should be reconsidered in any reformulation of trade union renewal, especially in labour market contexts that generate fragmentation and division among workers. The focus on the labour process as workers' day to day field of struggle is, at the same time, an antidote to institutionalization – a necessary strategy for trade unions to go beyond the logic of employment relations and the basis for developing workers' collective identity. I would say that the importance of these aspects lies in the counter-hegemonic discourse that they help to frame: identifying both an alternative and a strategy to follow. This seems particularly important when we consider that even grassroots forms of organizations, often forged by conflict and more prone actively to contest the status quo, have historically been trapped by contradictions similar to those experienced by traditional trade unions.

In this sense, following Darlington (1994) and his framework for shop stewards' actions, three contradictory tendencies may be identified: resistance/accommodation in relation to management, democracy/bureaucracy in relation to members and dependence/independence in relation to full-time union officials. However, 'each of these polar oppositions must be understood not as a fixed proposition in terms of an either/or logic but constantly in motion reflecting and at the same time changing the social conditions of which it is part' (Darlington 1994, p. 33). This motion and dynamism reflect not just of the shifting balance of power at the workplace but also the general opposition between classes at the level of society. As a result, the contradictory tendencies identified above will always appear in different combinations in relation to both general and specific conditions. However, in a system that reproduces conditions that favour and strengthen the power of capital:

> ... the most important factor pushing the balance of class forces in favour of the working class is their self-activity, organization and independent initiative through collective struggle in the workplace. It follows that the development of cohesive and self-confident shop steward organizations, able to apply pressure directly at the point of production, is a crucial factor in shifting the balance of workplace power and permitting further inroads into the prerogatives of capital (Darlington 1994, p. 34).

This emphasis on workplace structures as vehicles for the better defence of workers' interests, while not rejecting the necessity to use the institutional power of trade unions to gain advantages, is clearly a contribution to the existing debate on trade union renewal that goes in the same counter-hegemonic direction used by Gramsci in the idea of the factory councils. As recently argued by Cohen (2006) in her call to rebuild labour movement power, we do not need to look at a 'from above' vision of social movement unionism but rather at ways of strengthening the layer of militant activists born out of that 'grass-roots resistance *[that]* is almost always forthcoming at different times, in different sections, even in the most discouraging circumstances' (Cohen 2006, p. 2). In this perspective, what is required, then, is a democratically led organization that could develop horizontal structures, a class awareness and independence from capital – union as a movement rather than an institution.

While this vision of workers' organization and representation plays an important part in setting a counter-hegemonic discourse and practice, especially with respect to pluralist approaches to trade unionism and labour movement renewal, the contradictory tendencies in which even grassroots organizations are often trapped impose further reflections on the role, meaning and concrete possibility of forms of direct, democratic workplace unionism. What formal instruments should be used to guarantee participation in a context that constantly tends to divide workers in terms of skills and salary conditions? How to avoid the shift from militancy to bureaucracy in union leaderships? While grassroots-led mobilizations and the experience of struggle clearly lead to consciousness, how can this be maintained and the spaces for workers' participation widened? Following this, why then the issues of workers' control of the labour process and self-management are rarely considered in devising strategies for workers' action?

The construction of workers' representative organizations is fraught with difficulties and open to multiple determinants and opposing forces, with workers' bargaining power influenced by companies' active mobilization, by the role of the state or the level of techno-logical development and labour market segmentation. Reformist or revolutionary approaches to trade unionism that in turn reflect socio-political visions may add further complexity.

Because of all these complexities and the conflicting context of the capital-labour relationship, the history of workers' organizing has always been characterized by a pendulum swing between insti-tutionalisation and workers' emancipation, between a search for com-promise and recognition on the one hand and direct action on the other, reflecting power relations at the workplace and in society. This is nothing new, at least not for all those who see changes at work and improvements in labour conditions in dialectical terms along with working people's struggles. But paradoxically, what all these struggles have produced, by strengthening the organizational and institutional power of their representative organizations too, is the transformation of trade unions in a fetish. Thus, in terms of collective action, the mul-tiple expressions of workers' opposition to the rule of capital disappear and leave room only for trade unions' organized strikes. Discourses on workers' self-activity and self-management are normally dismissed. Participation in internal decision-making processes is reduced to rep-resentative democracy. Workers' power is built not on active oppos-ition and mobilization but in lobbying political parties.

The corollary to this situation, in which 'everything starts and finishes' with a trade union, is the mixed sense of impotence and pessimism produced on the moderate left by sharp declines in trade unions in the biggest industrial countries. Unfortunately, this has produced a further reformist approach, of which increased flexibility and precariousness for workers are just two aspects.

The approach of the research and the plan of the book

The debates presented in this introductory chapter set the broad the-oretical context in which studies of workers' struggles and collective action should be located. I have first considered the historical and theoretical determinations of workers' struggles. The structural antagonism and conflict of interests existing between capital and labour have in themselves the potentiality to produce spontaneous resistance. While this is a natural outcome of workplace relations, workers' collective action can have different forms and degrees of strength, depending, too, on the articulation of geographical, historical, technological and financial dynamics. This resistance often results in the constitution of collective organizations representing workers. Following from this, I have then considered the historical tendency of conflating all forms of collective action into the strike and consequently of establishing a model of 'institutionalized collective action' based on the logical association and sequence of industrial conflict, strikes and trade unions. In contrast to this, however, different geographical and historical experiences of workers' resistance point to their own capacities for mobilization and self-activity. In the third section of the chapter, I reconsidered this different approach to workers' collective action, by looking at the contradictory role of trade unions in alternately promoting and controlling bottom-up mobilization.

Overall, the approach used in this book rehabilitates a vision of collective action as a structurally determined and grassroots-based expression of workers' power. While the importance of leaders, established workers' organizations and political parties in building and strengthening workers' actions is often fundamental in counteracting capital's tendency to create divisions among workers, the repeated, spontaneous explosions of workers' resistance are testimony of their powers of self-organization.

Consequent with this approach, the second chapter presents what I have defined as a Marxist perspective on workers' collective action. There are three ways in which, I think, a Marxist perspective can be different from others: it aims to avoid subjective and individually based explanations, it focuses on the centrality of the capitalist labour process's contradictions in order to explain the nature of collective action and it gives the solidarity generated by cooperation in the labour process a key function in collectivizing workers' grievances. Following from this the chapter is organized into three sections. The first is a critique of Kelly's (1998) mobilization theory for the role he assigns to injustice, a leaders' framed subjective concept considered as the basis of any mobilization. The second, starting from this, explores Marx's insights into the nature of the capitalist labour process, in order to show how the latter internal dynamics produces both opportunities and constraints for collective action. In the third and final section, the chapter reconsiders the importance of solidarity in the light of its centrality in the labour process. Overall, through this reconstruction, the chapter intends to contribute to a Marxist perspective with a theory of collective action that is both theoretically solid and organizationally useful.

Chapter 3 presents an historical analysis of labour and social mobilization in Argentina during the period from the Second World War to the present with the idea of identifying trends that may have influenced the cases researched. Starting with the data collected during the fieldwork, three issues are considered, each in a different section of the chapter: military repression and its effects on workers' mobilization, the workers' attitude toward trade unionism and the socio-political context at the time of mobilization. The three sections give evidence of how in the history of the Argentine labour movement, in a context of politicization and class confrontations, workers' self-activity and organization have often produced spontaneous and leaderless mobilizations similar to one of the case studies presented later in the book. The recurrence of this type of collective action in the history of Argentina helps to establish an ideal link between the theoretical considerations presented in Chapter 2 and the empirical analysis of the cases of collective action studied in this research in Chapters 4 and 5.

Chapter 4 reconstructs in detail two different events of workers' mobilization, looking at the dynamics that provoked the workers' spontaneous occupation of FIAT's Ferreyra plant and the trade union-led occupation of CIADEA-Renault's Santa Isabel plant, both of which are located in the city of Córdoba. The two cases are compared not with the aim of establishing a best model for collective action, but to examine the roles of injustice and solidarity in the construction of collective action. Cases of spontaneous action evidence the different meanings that can be associated with the term injustice even within the same workplace and, most importantly, how flawed the concept is in theorizing collective action. Evidence is also provided to show how in the two cases different factors alternatively favoured and hindered the development of solidarity.

Following from this, Chapter 5 concentrates on an analysis of the events that occurred at FIAT in the year after the first occupation. In this case, considering an entire cycle of conflict and resistance from the perspectives of both the company and the workers, we can identify both the role of leadership and organization in strengthening solidarity and in the accompanying radicalization of workers and the company's repressive practices aimed at dividing workers and breaking solidarity.

In Chapter 6 I then reconsider the main findings and assumptions of the research to emphasize two aspects, in particular, that are both methodologically and theoretically important: the needs to look at collective action as a process and to approach it through a radical perspective. The fact that, empirically, many factors can potentially influence workers' potentialities for action does not necessarily imply that this is contingent in nature. Rather on the contrary, collective action develops, and this can be empirically proven, as a process that follows the contradictory dynamics of the capitalist labour process. Thus, from this perspective radical means both to go to the roots of the problem by using Marxists' insights into the nature of the labour process and to express a view of workers' self-organization that goes beyond trade unions as institutions.

2
A Marxist Perspective on Workers' Collective Action

Introduction

What drives workers periodically to contest their surrounding reality and how do they structure their protests? Providing answers to these crucial questions has always been at the centre of Marxist thinking and workplace research. Within this tradition there are key debates around structure and agency, and between subjective and objective conditions in the mobilizations of workers. This chapter aims to add to the theoretical debate and to militant action by proposing the reconstruction of a theory of workers' collective action rooted around four main pillars: the need to avoid subjective and individually based explanations, the centrality of the capitalist labour process' contradictions, the need to constantly demystify capital and the rediscovery of solidarity.

With this background in mind and drawing on previous work (Atzeni 2009), the chapter starts with a critique of Kelly's (1998) mobilization theory because of the role played in it by the concept of injustice – a subjective, individually framed concept considered the basis of any mobilization. The next section returns to the capitalist labour process that, in so far as it is the site of both capital valorization and worker cooperation, constantly creates contradictions, in terms of workers' opportunities and constrains on collective action. The final section makes a point for reconsidering solidarity as theoretically central, for being the social relation that expresses the collective nature of the labour process, and relevant as a tool for action and in workers' organizing.

Mobilization theory: a critique

After a decade of a research agenda dominated by human resource management (HRM) and assessments of work under it embedded in this ideologically driven paradigm, and in a context of labour and trade unions' retreat, the publication in 1998 of John Kelly's book, *Rethinking Industrial Relations: Mobilization, Collectivism and Long Waves*, represented a watershed in the field of industrial relations and labour studies.

For those approaching industrial relations in the tradition of the 1970s ethnographic workplace studies and the sociology of industrial action and trade unions, Kelly's work was important for two main reasons. First, it offered a theoretical framework for the study of the microdynamics of workplace conflict and for the understanding of waves of mobilization and counter-mobilization in a historical perspective. Second, by putting labour back to the centre stage, basing his analysis in the Marxist vision of society and arguing for the resilience of collectivism in a period of proclaimed individualism, it was a political call to counter-balance HRM dominated studies of work.

Because of its wide ranging perspective and critical approach, over the last decade the book became a must-read for all those interested in the study of labour organizing and collective action and the often cited Marxist-radical reference in the pluralist-dominated HRM.

Kelly's main argument, codified in what he calls mobilization theory, is that workplace social relations can be explored and collective action explained and fostered by studying the interrelations of a set of analytical categories: injustice, leadership, opportunity and organization. In the model, collective action is reconstructed as the final outcome of a process in which workers' generic feelings of injustice are transformed and made explicit by existing or natural leaders who attribute the causes of the injustice to the employer and, in presence of both a minimum of organizational structure and a strategic opportunity, call on workers to take action.

Each category and the overall model represent a powerful tool and departure point for empirical research in the analysis of the organizing strategies adopted by workers in cases of both mobilization and countermobilization. In recent years this has been reflected in a number of works that have used Kelly's framework in relation to leadership (Darlington 2007; 2001; 2002; Green, Black and Ackers

2000; Metochi 2002), unions' organizing (Gall 2000b; 2003; Kelly and Badigannavar 2005), injustice (Brown Johnson and Jarley 2004) and gender (Cox et al. 2007). Although these researchers have extended and tested empirically the theory, their conclusions do not put into question Kelly's main assumptions: that mobilization theory is based on injustice and that leaders are pivotal in framing this sense of injustice into a collective action.

Kelly's work has been already commented on in full detail (Gall 1999; 2000a), from different perspectives (for a review see Gall 2000a) and at different times (the most recent is Fairbrother 2005). In the following pages I am going to deal particularly with injustice, as I believe that it is crucial to uncover the subjectivity and individuality attached to the concept and thus its unsuitability for explaining collective phenomena.[1]

Despite Kelly's intellectual background and work in the Marxist tradition of industrial relations pervading his mobilization theory – constituting in itself a good theoretical antidote to any type of explanation purely based on subjective experiences – the centrality he assigns to injustice within the theory (*'the sine qua non of collective action'*, Kelly 1998, p. 27 and what 'should form the core intellectual agenda for industrial relations' Kelly 1998, p. 126) and particularly in framing workers' interests ('perceived injustice is the origin of workers' collective definition of interests', Kelly 1998, p. 64) is contradictory. On the one hand, it is made clear that workplace conflict is a feature of the antagonistic relations existing between workers and employers in the capitalist system and that because of this, two sets of diverging, often conflicting, interests emerge (Hyman 1975). On the other, it is giving theoretical relevance to a concept like that of injustice that is flawed both for its appeal to moral and ethical values and for its own indeterminacy.

As Gramsci argued, 'the concepts of equity and justice are merely formal...in a conflict each moral judgement is absurd because it can be based just on the same existing data that conflict tends to modify' (Gramsci 1991 p. 179, author's translation from Italian). Thus 'just' or 'unjust' are moral judgements and as such depend on the value and meaning each party in a conflict attaches to them. The concepts will reflect beliefs, realities and the power hegemonic relations of a specific society in a particular historical epoch. There will always be injustice; people will always feel aggrieved, exploited and unrewarded but the form of their injustice will never be the same. It is fair enough and common sense to think that people need a motivation to act but the problem will always be to determine the content of their feelings, if a link needs to be established with their mobilization. The moral value attached to injustice and its dependence on hegemonic ideology necessarily involves a definition of the concept not in absolute but in relative terms.

The use of concepts based on morality is always problematic, especially within a system, like that of capitalism, that appears to be founded on freedom while in reality generating coercion and that sees employer and worker relations in terms of mutual rights and obligations, while obscuring how unequal power struggles constantly change this reality. But this mystification is so strong that even workers engaged in struggle are trapped by the pervasiveness of morality. As Cohen argues,

> Clear-eyed awareness of capital as an unscrupulous class enemy is foreign to workers caught up in a passionate struggle in which they see right, and thus ultimately might, on their side. The notion that 'injustice' per se propels workers into struggle is put into question by most of the strike accounts in this book. (Cohen 2006, p. 206)

From this perspective, once we think about the unquestioned morality of workplace relations, assumptions taken for granted (management's right to manage, capitalist justifications for efficiency and productivity, redistribution of losses but centralization of profits and market logic's overwhelming presence) occupy the stage, making questions of justice/injustice almost senseless. Here in the workplace is indeed where that change in the *dramatis personae* to which Marx referred finally occurs and where the worker 'is timid and holds back, like someone who has brought his own hide to the market and now has nothing else to expect but – a tanning' (Marx 1976, p. 280).

It is worth asking then, within a system that constantly mystifies, how many times workers, everywhere in the world, have had to tolerate some form of injustice? Did they always mobilize or we have to think, as Moore (1978) argued, that they accepted the inevitable?[2] What is the link between their individual feelings of injustice and collective mobilization? Clearly, a theory that wants to explain collective phenomena starting from a subjectively determined, morally grounded, basis is deeply flawed.

This problem remains, and is probably reinforced, exactly because real life very often confronts us with collective grievances framed within injustice. Thus injustice appears as the flag of new social movements and labour alliances (Waterman and Wills 2001); it is considered functional to a renewal of trade unionism in the 'organising unionism' perspective (Heery 2002), is a valid target for NGO/ trade unions' joint campaigns (Ellis 2004) and, more in general, is certainly useful as concept for framing grievances. It is fair to think that, together with a mobilization, there should be a cognitive moment, a communication and an exchange of ideas among workers within which injustice is framed. As Gall (2000a) suggests, workers should feel confident, and there should be a surrounding context favourable for action. Yet these are factors that may influence a mobilization but are not the necessary conditions.

In the sphere of political proposal and organization, injustice maintains a catalysing function in summarizing in one single powerful word the anger of many. It is in this sense very useful as a concept used by leaders in unifying the discontented. But this perspective may be easily substituted by other moral value-based concepts performing a similar cohesive function (e.g. dignity, inequality or fairness) or by leaders' appeals to local traditions of labour antagonism and cultural diversity/ opposition to the employer. Thus the problem it is not to deny the existence of injustice in the everyday discourse of labour and political leaders or to deny that workers may really feel a situation is unjust, but rather, that the focus on injustice as the conceptual basis for mobilization, for the argument that we have developed so far, is theoretically flawed and reinforces the idea that collective action in the workplace is all about contesting rights instead of power and class relations.

The simultaneous obscuration of class relations and conceptual upgrading of injustice to being the basis for mobilization does not produce a general theory of collective action but a theoretical framework for action functional to unions' organizing. Although injustice is considered as the *conditio sine qua non* of mobilization, leaders, indeed, are pivotal: they are in charge of moulding injustice, attributing this to the employer and convincing workers to organize and take action.

It cannot be denied that mobilization often follows this sequence and that leaders always play a central role in it, but we should also account for those cases of spontaneous, all-of-a-sudden, mobilizations in which no preconditions could be detected and where leaders do not play any fundamental role. The recent experience of factory occupations in post-crisis Argentina (Atzeni and Ghigliani 2007a) is a good example of this trend. Workers occupied their factories spontaneously, without any previous organization or militant activity, because no other options were available in the market. Structural conditions forced them to react and, surprisingly for any vanguard theory, they did it without any conscious preparatory work but in a very revolutionary way: by challenging property rights, producing under workers' control and redistributing income equally.

Furthermore, how many times we have witnessed mobilizations outside union channels or with bureaucratic leaderships forced by the mass to take action? How many times do these types of mobilizations go unnoticed? How many times do systems of industrial relations impose rules that divide workers and transform the exercise of collective action into a never-ending fulfilment of procedures?

A theory of workers' collective action within the Marxist tradition would never be a definitive account, as new forms, times and conditions for action will constantly be reinvented, often in the course of the same struggle. But it should be able to identify the structural conditions that both promote and repress workers' action and with this demystify the overall system of assumptions that governs labour-capital relations. This means in turn a need to return to the labour process, as that is the site where both the opposition of labour to capital and, yet, its dependence on it are constantly reproduced and solidarity linkages are established.

A return to the labour process

Marx was clear in showing that the particular nature of the commodity labour, its inseparability from the worker, imposed a first, natural, obstacle to its free consumption by capitalists. In order to benefit fully from what they bought in the market and to ensure that labour power was transformed into concrete productive labour, capitalists had to find methods to control, direct and discipline workers.

> Through the co-operation of numerous wage-labourers, the command of capital develops into a requirement for carrying on the labour process itself, into a real condition of production. That a capitalist should command in the field of production is now as indispensable as that a general should command on the field of battle. (Marx 1976, p. 448)

But, just as generals in a war need to strengthen their control and impose tougher discipline on their troops, so capitalists have to engage in a constant struggle to increase the surplus value generated by the workers through the production process.

> The driving motive and determining purpose of capitalist production is the self-valorization of capital to the greatest possible extent, i.e. the greatest possible production of surplus-value, hence the greatest possible exploitation of labour power by the capitalist. (Marx 1976, p. 449)

Further, because the drive to valorization will be completed once the product of labour is sold on the market and because under free competition, the immanent law of capitalist production confronts the individual capitalist as a coercive force external to him (Marx 1976, p. 381), capitalists will need to organize production and capture surplus labour in a way that can make them more efficient and thus more profitable than their competitors.

Thus, from the point of view of our employer, the labour process is contemporaneously a process of production and valorization driven by competition and, as such, imposes on him/her first the need to find methods, through the organization of the production process and the control of it, to capture and embody in commodities the highest possible amount of surplus labour produced by workers, and then to transform this into surplus value through exchange on the market. Considering that the full realization of capital, and the possibility of its reproduction, requires both production and exchange, the two levels will always be interconnected, with direct consequences for workers. Crises of profitability generated in the market are indeed immediately 'solved' by individual employers restructuring their production processes either by introducing new technology, intensifying and rationalizing the use of workers' time or simply by cutting labour costs through reducing wages, introducing flexibility, using or threatening outsourcing and moving production or making people redundant.

Because the nature of capital's imperative is valorization and competition acts on individual capitalists as an immanent and coercive law, the interests of the employers, individually and as a class, will always tend to conflict with those of the workers. In fact no matter how good or bad the employer, how short- or long-term his/

her business perspective, workers will be confronted by a system of rules, control, discipline and time management – at the point of production and structured around the need to guarantee profitability – that sooner or later will appear and act coercively on them. At the same time, due to their dependence on a wage to live, any changes to their standard of living, through direct wage reduction, unemployment or an increase in the price of basic commodities, will be evidence of their interests not being satisfied within the existing system.

This perspective on interests evidences once again, the interconnectedness of production and valorization within the capitalist labour process and the need to look at it as a unity. As Cohen argues:

> the issues of valorization and exploitation – the structuring of the organization of labour by the objective of valorization, with its accompanying pressure for reduction of socially necessary labour time, and the contradictions centring on exploitation to which this give rise – surface routinely at the point of production as conflicts of interests between workers and management. (Cohen 1987, p. 7)

For our understanding of workers' mobilization, the contradictory and conflicting nature of the capitalist labour process, as an organization of production driven by valorization, is crucial. Spontaneous, unexpected, unorganized forms of resistance, the sudden mobilizations of previously loyal workers and the transformation of apparently economistic types of conflict into political ones are all forms of mobilization that can be explained just by reference to the existence of a structure that constantly produces conditions for conflict. The same structure that has justified the historical appearance of trade unions as organizations representing workers' interests explains the existence of daily routine struggles at the point of production between workers and management. In this latter context, workers may have been forced to accept a particular system of authority and control, and may have found ways of accommodating and even cooperating with it (Burawoy 1979).[3] But it is not control and authority per se that generates resistance; it is a company's constant drive for profitability within a competitive system that everyday jeopardizes the scope for consensus, transforming previously accepted practices of management control into an unbearable invasion into workers' lives.

> The control exercised by the capitalist is not only a special function arising from the nature of the social labour process, and peculiar to that process, but it is at the same time a function of the exploitation of a social labour process, and is consequently conditioned by the unavoidable antagonism between the exploiter and the raw material of his exploitation. (Marx 1976, p. 449)

Workers' potential for resistance and the structuring of their interests, as opposed to those of their employers, can be placed, from a theoretical perspective, within the dynamics of production-valorization-competition. But this does not guarantee the immanence of conflict in real social life, rather the contrary. For workers, living in a capitalist society means not just confrontation and clashes with capital's imperative at the point of production, not simply engagement in struggles at the workplace over the 'frontier of control', over the labour-wage bargaining, but also being forced to sell their own labour in a labour market that individuals cannot control and being dependent on wages to live. These coercive conditions are natural, taken for granted, and exploitation – in terms of extraction of surplus value – is not part of the workers' daily vocabulary. Capital creates a society that appears to be based on freedom and equality. Workers exchange their labour for an average wage; they exchange commodities for commodities in the market. The capitalists buy the right to consume the commodity labour, put the workers together to work, add the means of production to the production process and thus 'legally' appropriate the fruits of social labour, returning to the market for the final realization of profit. Every improvement in society is then attributable to capital; exploitation disappears, society depends on capital and workers depend on capital, until the point at which:

> workers are not simply dependent upon the state of capital in general for their jobs and thus their ability to satisfy their needs; they are dependent on particular capitals! Precisely because capital exists in the form of many capitals, and those capitals compete against each other to expand, there is a basis for groups of

workers to link their ability to satisfy their needs to the success of those particular capitals that employ them. In short, even without talking about the conscious effort of capital to divide, we can say that there exists a basis for the separation of workers in different firms – both inside and between countries. (Lebowitz 2004, p. 4)

Our analysis of the structural conditions promoting mobilization could stop at this point. Workers do not only appear to be, but really are dependent on capital to survive and they tend to find ways of accommodating themselves to it. More than this, their dependence on particular capitals, which operate in constant competition, creates the conditions for a permanent separation and division of workers. However, at different times and places, but continuously, they engage in struggles against the system that is exploiting them. Why? Because the capitalist labour process, simultaneously a production and valorization process, is inherently contradictory. When the impelling need of capitalists for profitability breaks even the illusion of an equal exchange relation, exploitation is revealed. Changes in workers' everyday working conditions (longer hours, harder work or greater danger), despotic managerial control (less freedom of movement, tighter definition of tasks or separation of workers), reduction of wages and redundancies are some of the forms in which this exploitation is represented.

But considering workers' mobilization as a simple reaction to capital's logic would reduce all conflicts to a matter of wage negotiation and consequently would overemphasize the economistic function, and consciousness, of trade unions. It is certainly true that in the majority of cases conflicts find a temporary solution in a monetary agreement and that systems of industrial relations find in collective bargaining about wages the key for a compromise between capital and labour. But workers struggle not just about money but also about their conditions as human beings.

> It is quite unrealistic to suppose that because a worker works only for money he accordingly shuts off his mind to his daily experiences at the factory. If he treats his labour as a commodity it does not follow that he expects himself, as a person, to be treated as a commodity. Neither does it follow that he will be prepared to put up with anything if the money is right. (Lane and Roberts 1971, p. 228)

It is a question of freedom as against control and authority, the creativity of each individual as against the dehumanization produced by machines and the existence of fully developed human beings as against alienation.

> The arrangements of technology and authority require unthinking obedience. Little wonder then that wildcat strikers sometimes talk as if they have 'done something big for the first time in their lives'. Such people are proclaiming their humanity and protesting that their work situation denies it. (Lane and Roberts 1971, p. 232)

The contradictions of the capitalist labour process create then two different but converging and overlapping sets of motivations for workers to struggle. The first, more evident, set aims to reforms workers' material conditions within the existing system. The importance of these struggles should not be underestimated. First of all, as has been empirically proven – the research in this book representing a further example of this – the workers who have passed thorough a process of struggle and mobilization return to normal life as different, more conscious persons. Second, conflict that begins over typical bread and butter issues may easily grow in intensity and extend to more radical ones in a context of increasing social and political relevance. Third, these struggles help the formation and establishment of new grassroots forms of organization and more democratically oriented leadership, thus promoting a more militant and more active participation. The second set of motivations refers more to what Lebowitz (2003) calls the 'worker's own need for development'. Within a system that constantly creates new, unfulfilled, needs for workers',

> workers are engaged in a constant struggle against capital – struggles to reabsorb those alien and independent products of their activity, struggles to find time and energy for themselves, struggle propelled by their own need for development. (Lebowitz 2003, p. 204)

Thus workers are not just the passive subjects of capital's imperative for profit, but have an active role in transforming the system that exploits them:

> no worker known to historians ever had surplus value taken out of his hide without finding some way of fighting back (there are

plenty of ways of going slow); and paradoxically, by his fighting back the tendencies were diverted and the forms of development were themselves developed in unexpected ways. (Thompson 1978, pp. 345–46, cited in Harvey 2006, p. 115)

Reconsidering the workers' side in explaining their resistance to capitalism has important consequences. First it moves us away from a deterministic reconstruction of the social reality and toward a possibility for social change directly interrelated with the Marxist concept of praxis. Workers' practical activities and experiences gained in the struggle for material benefits are thus essential because through these struggles, while changing their conditions, they change themselves. Second, and a corollary to this, a theory of workers' collective action cannot be reduced either to strategies or to a social psychological account, but should, first of all, reveal and communicate the inner nature of the mystification of capital. Third, it talks about changes in technology and the organization of the production process as being driven by both the law of competition and workers' pressure. It is because workers depend on capital to survive, but capital also depends on workers for profitability that management and workers will alternate moments of compromise and peace with resistance. This introduces a dynamic element into the understanding of workers' resistance and the historical formation of the working class and helps to reject a trade union-based pessimistic view regarding the possibility for social change.

We have started this section by highlighting how the contradictions inherent in the capitalist labour process constantly generate exploitation, recreating the structure from which conflict can emerge. But the capitalist labour process, like any other labour process intended as creative human activity, is not just the site of exploitation per se, but also the site of cooperation. In fact, despite the tendency to divide workers, to segment work and to separate mental from manual work, the production process imposes at least a minimum level of cooperation. If on the one hand this cooperation becomes functional to capital's valorization, on the other it represents a first associational moment among the collective of workers, upon which solidarity links may be created. Thus in a search for a theory of collective action, the relations between cooperation, solidarity and workers' collective action need to be explored further.

Cooperation, solidarity and workers' collective action

The cooperation that necessarily takes place in the capitalist labour process is inherently contradictory. On the one hand, the workers 'as co-operators, as members of a working organism, they merely form a particular mode of existence of capital. Hence the productive power developed by the worker socially is the productive power of capital' (Marx 1976, p. 451). But on the other, 'As the number of the co-operating workers increases, so too does their resistance to the domination of capital, and, necessarily, the pressure put on by capital to overcome this resistance' (Marx 1976, p. 449).

How could workers, whose cooperation is a function of capital and who depend on capital to survive, develop a resistance to it? And in contrast, why should managerial strategies always tend to divide workers and create competition among them? Key to these answers is workers' change of consciousness. Through cooperation at work the individual worker starts to develop a consciousness of her/himself not just as individual but also as part of a group who share similar working conditions, who demand better salaries and job protection and whose interests are overall opposed to those of the employer. The collective labourer, in Marx's term, takes then the scene, reshaping the individuality attached to the labour-wage exchange relation into the collective nature of the labour process.

For the collective labourer, while cooperation at work is the material condition, creating room for communication and exchange among workers, solidarity is the social relation that expresses the collective nature of the labour process. Any fruitful attempts to explain workers' resistance must thus depart from the centrality that solidarity has both theoretically and in the practical, militant discourse.

Stressing this point is even more important when the social sciences, as the society overall, are invaded by commonsense perspectives like the one that considers a minimum level of solidarity as a basic condition for any collective action. As an implicit consequence of taking solidarity for granted, the attention of researchers has been focused on the identification of preconditions for collective action on which solidarity can develop. As a result solidarity is explained as a function, for instance, of social networks, of a powerful leadership, of the organizational strength of trade unionism, generally confusing cause with effect.

We should start by inverting the analysis: it is because a form of solidarity pre-exists that other organizational developments can follow. The simple fact that labour is a collective activity, implying for workers the need to perform an activity together, generates a sense of mutual dependency and a need for support: the embryonic form of solidarity, or what can be called 'solidarity not yet activated'. This unity has a very practical nature, it is just to perform the job, but it is also the first step in the recognition: (a) that the employer has the power to order the forms and times for the execution of the work and (b) that who gives this order is by, their very nature, on the other side, opposed and this despite the need for workers to be accommodated within the system. This twofold recognition represents in turn a qualitative step in each worker's consciousness, gradually transforming individual identities into collective ones. This process – which is generated and presupposed by the solidarity built into the cooperative, yet contradictory, nature of the capitalist labour process – is fundamental not just in strengthening workplace-based solidarities, those oppositional and spontaneous 'cultures of solidarity' to which Fantasia (1988) refers to, but also in creating the basis for those forms of collective sharing or dialogical democracy that Offe and Wiesenthal consider as the necessary moments for workers to mediate between their contrasting individual and collective interests.

> The logic of collective action of the relatively powerless differs from that of the relatively powerful in that the former implies a paradox that is absent from the latter – the paradox that *interests can only be met to the extent they are partly redefined*. (Offe and Wiesenthal 1980, p. 79, emphasis in the original)

Without the recognition of solidarity as the foundational moment of collective action, we cannot understand the real basis for the success of union activity, the need for workers to be organized, political calls for workers' unity and, in contrast, all the cases of spontaneous mobilization beyond the union channel or in deunionized workplaces.

Conflict and collective action emerge not just by virtue of external forces but because there is an existing fertile soil in the form of the embryonic solidarity described above. In this sense, social networks, group or class identification, perceptions of injustice and leaders' actions, despite their importance in collective action, do not represent a *conditio sine qua non* of this solidarity. Instead, they should be understood as vehicles for the circulation and confirmation of it, as elements able to activate a pre-existing embryonic form of solidarity.

By assuming that solidarity is a social relation expressed by the collective nature of the labour process and thus the objective basis of mobilization, we are identifying an abstract, but nonetheless real, concrete minimum for its definition and can observe how dominant social relations produce conditions that alter and modify this basic experience and thus the possibility for solidarity to reach its second level of development, or its 'active' form.

These assumptions have an almost natural corollary in the methods we should use to identify solidarity empirically, and in its conceptualization. What I propose here is to think of solidarity as a concept that can best be perceived as a dynamic process and should be analysed in 'progress'. We cannot simply measure, detect and search for preconditions of solidarity. This does not necessarily imply the empirical identification of it. There may be preconditions that are considered good indicators of an already developed form of solidarity (class consciousness, previous struggles and organization), but these are by no means a guarantee of future mobilizations. On the contrary, we may have mobilizations born out of situations that did not show on the surface any positive indicator of solidarity. Questions such as when and why solidarity occurs, or what are the reasons/agents for its development into an active form, can be addressed only through an analysis of solidarity in different moments of its development.

By insisting on searching for solidarity as a static reality we will end up in a vicious circle pretending to offer concrete, objective signs of its existence (because without it we cannot even think of collective action) but without considering how structural conditions affect it. The implicit consequence of this mechanism is to consider solidarity almost like a transcendental, evanescent concept that exists but is difficult to investigate empirically (for instance Fantasia 1995; Portelli 1991) and is, however, easily adaptable to a wide variety of studies: labour process (Beynon 1984; Edwards and Scullion 1982), class consciousness (Fantasia 1988; Rosendahl 1985) and cultural and historical accounts of the working class (Bruno 1999, Hanagan 1980).

However, the excess of taxonomy that in the social sciences often creates the problems of definition and classification mentioned above does not seem to affect workers. A review of historical conflicts from the perspective of those directly involved reveals that their concerns are not about the meaning and existence of solidarity but rather about the possibility of creating and consolidating it in presence of employers', management's, governments' or trade union bureaucracy's attempts to break it (for Argentina this may be found in the historical accounts of 1970s and 1960s workers' militancy in the city of Córdoba in Brennan 1994; Gordillo 1999; James 1988). Workers do not need to search for a definition or to look for solidarity's preconditions. They simply have a living encounter with solidarity, a sense of empowerment when it becomes manifest and drives their action forward or a sense of disappointment and anger when it does not appear, leaving room for divisions and individualism. Just as capitalist exploitation is hidden by the wage relation so solidarity is hidden by the legitimacy of the command of capital in the workplace and workers' dependency on their salaries to live.

This inescapable condition of dependency does not just hinder the possibility of building on solidarity but it also tends to create, as we have seen before, groups of workers fully identified with the particular capital employing them and proud of the quality of their work.

> A fundamental loyalty to the value of production for use rather than exchange, concrete rather than abstract labour, emerges in the bewildered resentment of many workers over their replacement by 'unskilled' workers in a strike, or the transfer of their jobs abroad, despite what for them is the crucial component of worker knowledge and 'quality' of work. (Cohen 2006, p. 194)

All of these problems make it extremely risky to establish when and how solidarity will assume its 'active' form, as this depends on the combination, at a certain time, of the forms of labour-capital opposition in the workplace and in society as a whole. Unfortunately, we do not yet have a theory of collective action precise enough to predict the future. What we can do is to indicate on the map the cardinal points for theoretical and empirical analysis, and solidarity can be considered as one of these points.

Putting solidarity back at the centre stage of our understanding of collective action is to contribute to a theoretical, as well as a political, debate. The concept of solidarity has been distorted by decades of ideological and rhetorical use. Yet, once we reframe this concept within the structural contradictions generated by labour-capital relations in the workplace and the overwhelming dominance of capital in society, we are contributing to its demystification and contesting taken-for-granted assumptions about work and 'modern' ways of life. Once put in this context, the emphasis on solidarity may be able to provide workers with a clearer understanding of their potential strength and rank and file organizations with a more concrete, everyday, basis for militant discourse and action.

Conclusions and implications for empirical analysis

This chapter's overall aim has been to offer a reconstruction of workers' collective action from a Marxist perspective. Without pretending to be exhaustive and exegetic in its approach, the chapter has been developed by using Marx's insights into the nature of the capitalist labour process and into the hidden truths of the dominant conceptions of work and the political economy. Four main assumptions follow from this background, influencing the chapter's overall reconstruction of collective action. First, attempts to look at workers' collective action as the sum of individuals and as driven by subjective determinations of social reality, like the one associated with injustice, are theoretically wrong and misleading and do not explain the variety and complexity of workers' actions. Injustice may be a useful tool for trade unions' organizing and revitalization but it is framed within capital's fetishism. Second and consequent to this, a demystification of the system governing the overall labour-capital relations in the workplace and society is fundamental. Third, through this demystification it is possible to discover the inherent contradictions of the capitalist labour process generating both resistance and accommodation. Fourth, a theory that aims to communicate and strengthen knowledge among workers and their rank and file organizations of the constraints and opportunities for collective action needs, once the reality of the capitalist labour process is unveiled, to reconsider the role of solidarity and its potentialities in framing organizational strategies. Conscious rank and file militants and intellectuals supporting the labour movement should then constantly find ways of breaking capital's rule by demystifying it. In this sense, the emphasis on solidarity is fundamental, for both theory and organizational practice.

Can we use the theoretical insights developed in this chapter for the analysis of concrete cases of workers' mobilization? How can we account for the complexity and multiple determinants of collective actions by emphasizing just the contradictions of the capitalist labour process and the solidarity built into workers' cooperation? How can we explain the role of leaders and organizations, for instance, in building and strengthening workers' mobilization?

The answer to these questions is not straightforward and implies decisions about our methods and approach to research. We may be interested in proposing a theory for analysis and for action that responds to specific categories and is sequential like the one proposed by Kelly in his mobilization theory, rooted in the injustice-leadership-collective action framework. In this, it is taken for granted that the capitalist labour process generates conflict and that necessary conditions for workers' mobilization are already set within the system. The theory thus offers a clear set of conditions for action that researchers can use and test and activists may consider in the reorientation and rethinking of their strategies. Another approach is to enter into the complexity of the social dynamics that produce workers' mobilization by starting from a reformulation and reproposition of the conditions that constantly generate the basic antagonism between capital and labour. This approach, while reusing and reformulating Marx's concepts, is at the same time intellectually fundamental to demystifying the system of appearances produced by capitalism and methodologically valid for explaining the complexity of workers' collective actions. Empirically, the combination of many different factors, each important on its own, can contribute to explaining why workers have mobilized in a specific case. From favourable external socio-political conditions to internal organizational strength, from management violation of rules to workers' explicit confrontational strategy, from charismatic leadership to political parties guiding mobilization, from grassroots to bureaucracy-led mobilization, from mobilization under the banner of injustice to action in solidarity with other organizations, from planned mobilizations to spontaneous ones, all these are just examples of some of the factors that either alone or in combination influence workers' decisions to act collectively. But each factor's relevance within specific cases would be lost if the complexity in the understanding of workers' collective action were not placed within a parallel understanding of the structural conditions imposed by a system that constantly generates 'material relations between persons and social relations between things' (Marx 1976, p. 166). The insistence throughout the whole chapter on the capitalist labour process as the site where appearance and reality are, at the same time, contradictorily created is fundamental in this perspective.

Overall the approach used in this research, while acknowledging the importance of specific factors like leadership or organization, tries to avoid contingent and subjectively based reconstructions of collective action starting from the definition of the necessary conditions to promote mobilization. This is essential both in terms of defining a generally applicable theory and in terms of methods as it promotes an analysis in the making of the social processes leading to mobilization. We need to start from the contradictions of the capitalist labour process – from the objective structural conditions of mobilization – to observe in the empirical analysis how the existence of solidarity is contemporaneously obscured from and revealed to workers. Theory cannot go further than indicating the possibility for an alternative within the system and the importance, in the interest of workers' emancipation, to struggle for it. After all, praxis remains the best antidote against determinism.

Keeping in consideration the theoretical and methodological approach proposed in this chapter, the rest of the book will be dedicated to reconstruct in details two different cases of workers' mobilization occurred in two cars' plants of Córdoba, Argentina during 1996–97. The following chapter will set the cases in context by looking in historical perspective at a range of factors that may have influenced workplace mobilization in Argentina.

3

The Roots of Mobilization: Workplace and Social Conflict in Argentina in an Historical Perspective

Introduction

This chapter presents an historical background for the analysis of mobilization. Consequently, attention is drawn to those aspects of Argentine social history and trade unionism that could help to explain the cases of mobilization in this research. Can we identify recurring trends and how do these influence our interpretation of events? The analysis, starting from the data collected during the fieldwork, looks, in particular, at those historical or contextual factors that the workers interviewed have indicated in the interviews as being main obstacles in the process of mobilization and/or in the radicalization of it. Three thematic and recurrent issues have been identified: military repression and its effects on worker mobilization, the workers' attitude toward trade unionism and the socio-political context at the time of mobilization. In line with this the chapter has been organized into three main sections. The first reconsiders how the use of repressive practices, adopted systematically by military governments in Argentina until 1983, affected workers' potential for mobilization. Although these practices have clearly produced a loss in terms of organizational structure, increased by the large-scale assassination of delegates and activists as under the last military dictatorship, workers have nonetheless mobilized, often in spontaneous, unorganized ways. The second investigates the complexity and contradictions within the Argentine trade union movement, simultaneously the political backbone of the Peronist movement, an institutional actor and the representative of working class interests. These multiple identities have often been in conflict, giving room, within a rigid, state controlled system of workers' representation, for spontaneous grassroots types of worker mobilization and intra-union conflicts – expressions of workers' opposition to both employers and trade unions' rigid bureaucratic structure. The third section puts the case studies in the socio-political context that dominated in the 1990s, the time of the events considered. During that decade, the adoption of the neo-liberal model promoted by Menem, a Peronist president, had devastating effects for workers, with rising unemployment, worsening working conditions, increased productivity with the use of flexibility and a reduction of real wages. Trade unions, pressed between the need to offer answers to workers' discontent and their loyalty to a Peronist government offered weak and late reactions, once more creating the conditions for workers' struggles outside the union channel.

We could argue that in the history of the Argentine labour movement, in a highly politicized context of strong class conflict, this type of non-union, often spontaneous, leaderless mobilization, has been very important, and we can find examples of this in the case studies analysed in the following chapters. Although statistically uncounted, less frequent and overall numerically inferior to traditional trade union-led mobilizations, workers' collective struggles can assume spontaneous, unorganized forms whose importance transcends simple empirical considerations. Those cases of direct action that occur in the absence of an organizational agent are those that most powerfully show the structural conditions of workers' collective action in the terms presented in the theoretical chapter.

The three sections in which the chapter is organized are preceded by a chronological table (Table 3.1) that lays out key events/trends in the social and industrial relations history of Argentina. Table 3.1 aims to introduce readers to the specific issues treated in more detail all through the chapter and it is thus not exhaustive.

Table 3.1   A chronology of major events in Argentine social and industrial relations history, 1943–2008

Year	Major events
1943	Military government – Perón head of the *Secretaría de Trabajo y Previsión* – start of the process of juridification of industrial relations
1945	General strike in support of Perón, regulation of trade union representation, *personería gremial*
1946	Perón elected president, compulsory participation of public authorities in collective agreements
1946–1952	Continue process of juridification of industrial relations with parallel development of shop steward structures, *comisiones internas*
1952–1955	Perón elected president for the second time, declining capital profitability and increased role of comisiones internas
1955–1958	Military government, Perón exiled, anti-labour legislation and workplace resistance, *Resistencia Peronista*
1958–1962	Civil government under Frondizi, state recognition of central trade union organizations, emphasis on collective bargaining but also recognition of plant unions (FIAT's SITRAC and SITRAM) to curb industrial union power
1963–1966	Civil government under Arturo Illia, 1964 CGT *Plan de Lucha* with 11,000 factories occupied
1966–1969	Military government, under Onganía, repression of workers, suspension of collective bargaining, attempt to introduce a multi-union model to reduce the importance of central and workplace-based organizations
1969	*Córdobazo*, general strike and popular rebellion led by left-wing trade unions in the streets of Córdoba. Onganía forced to resign
1970–1973	New military governments with Levingston and Lanusse, repression of workers and anti-labour policies continue, the return of Perón is negotiated. Another rebellion in Córdoba, Viborazo, emergence of so-called *clasista* trade unions at FIAT with SITRAC/SITRAM, 1970/71 and Renault with SMATA, 1972
1973–1976	Return of Perón and second presidency, trade unions co-opted into government, peak level for real salaries in 1974, strong opposition to economic reforms led by both national trade unions and shop stewards organization networks, *coordinadoras*
1976–1983	Military government, concerted attack on trade union structures, financial power and workplace organizations. Assassination of militants and workers, clandestine opposition through sabotage and low level strikes

Continued

Table 3.1 Continued

Year	Major events
1983–1989	Civil government under Alfonsín, attempts to reform trade union representation and introduce unpopular economic policies opposed by the CGT, 13 general strikes
1989–1995	Hyperinflation and full implementation of neo-liberal economic policies, privatizations, labour flexibility, trade union fragmentation creation of CTA, MTA, attempts to decentralize collective bargaining
1995–1999	Rising unemployment and informal sector, four general strikes against flexibility, trade union action scattered and dispersed, weakened workplace organizations, radicalization of social conflict at national and local level
1999–2001	New president, de la Rúa (radical), follows similar economic policies, deep recession, increased importance of social mobilization and the movement of the unemployed, trade unions play a secondary role
2001–2002	Economic and social turmoil, de la Rúa resigns, widespread social mobilization, experiences of workers' self-management in 200 recovered factories
2003–2008	Economy starts to grow again, government promotes tripartite agreements and collective bargaining for social cohesion, reunification of CGT, new labour conflicts for wages increases, emergence of grassroots mobilizations initially tolerated and then repressed by Kirchner government

Military repression and workers' mobilization

Those who were militants and who had a voice among us are all gone, they have disappeared, they have been killed, they were simply not there anymore. Unfortunately all those, like me, who remained, now I can say, for cowardice, for necessity, for the family, for whatever reason, we never had the strength, the capability [...] we disagreed but we did not act, we disagreed but at the end we did all it was ordered to do by bending the head [...] an entire generation has grown without those leaders able to unify people, leaders respected by the rest. When the new fellows came to work they could just see our examples and this meant for them to see people always nodding the head and saying yes.

(Renault white collar worker)[4]

Argentina is like this ... 'do not get yourself into trouble', 'let's go fight together but better you go first', this society has been severely punished during the epoch of the military so people fear to expose themselves. You have seen what happened last year in Buenos Aires for the protest against the corralito, there was repression and people dead. Because of this, people remain fearful that something can happen to them if they protest.[5]

(Renault production worker)

I have always tried to maintain myself capable of thinking and this is what, in these years, has been removed from people's minds ... here we still have a clear image of what the dictatorship represented and this will be very difficult to change ... here there is no participation.[6]

(FIAT production worker)

These quotations represent just a sample of a recurrent issue concerning the heritage of the last military dictatorship on mobilization and worker solidarity. The interviews allow us to depict a picture in which military repression and the climate of terror thus created appear as the direct or indirect causes of a number of factors that have hampered mobilization and have broken solidarity and participation among workers. Put together, these factors are a generalized fear of being exposed to violent reaction, the destruction of activism leaving no combative examples/leaders for the new generation of workers, a tendency to individualism both within plants and in relation to other workers' struggles, no participation in society and no interest in politics.

The validity of these factors and their generalization are highly debatable. But whether or not we consider them true or false and applicable to other cases, it still remains important that many workers have indicated such factors as being direct or indirect consequences of the military dictatorship on their mobilization and solidarity behaviour. There is in oral history and interviews a dimension of knowledge that although not objectively true is still rich in information about the contexts, where the same protagonists of events could have been, at the time, involuntary subjects of representations. This is what Portelli (1991) calls the *'different credibility'* of oral history, the possibility of extracting from the representation of facts not in adherence with reality the meanings that actors have attached to it.

In order better to evaluate the meanings and the reality workers have described we will draw examples concerning their attitudes under the last military dictatorship, as well as from other cases under both authoritarian and non-authoritarian governments. Anticipating some conclusions we could say that it remains doubtful if the last period of military rule really was a watershed in hampering worker mobilization and introducing a generalized passivity among Argentine workers. This could be argued especially if we look at the high level of mobilization that occurred in the decades after, and even during, the period of military government. But at the same time it seems undeniable that part of the reality also coincides with FIAT and Renault workers' points of view.

If we look at waves of mobilization in Argentina during military and authoritarian governments prior to that of 1976–83, we can conclude that repression and dictatorship have produced radicalization and uprisings at both plant and societal levels instead of the fear, lack of solidarity and search for individualistic solutions as seems to emerge from the interviews. In 1969 the city of Córdoba, as well as Rosario and other inland industrial agglomerations, was the major site of a popular revolutionary uprising against the government of General Onganía and the economic and labour policies he was implementing. In the context of Córdoba, a newly industrialized city developed around the labour-intensive automotive industry and with a tradition of independent trade unionism, military repression acted as a catalyst for mobilization. If we look at the dynamics of the *Córdobazo*, that mobilization started as a traditional workers' protest, with marches to the city centre, against the government's decision to cancel the *Sábado Inglés*, a shortening of the working day on Saturdays that had traditionally been granted to workers. But social support and solidarity at that time and the homogeneity of the working class helped to identify in the dictatorship the common enemy and to transform a labour protest into revolutionary mobilization[7] (Brennan 1994; Delich 1970; Gordillo 1999). In the same city two years later another protest, similar to the *Córdobazo*, the *Viborazo*,[8] occurred and both were determining factors in the removal from power of first General Onganía and then General Levingston, who at the time of these events were presidents of Argentina.

In June and July 1975 another wave of mobilizations and general strikes affected the country. At that time the armed forces were not directly involved in the government, but the repression and physical disappearance of militant workers and the takeover by the authorities of independent unions were common features.[9] The state of fear and terror created by the activities of the AAA[10] (Argentine Anticommunist Alliance) and the obstacles to mobilization imposed on workers by the central union bureaucracies, did not prevent collective action, and worker mobilizations were often part of a broader political confrontation between left and right sectors within Peronism and in the whole of Argentine society (Thompson 1982). At that time Peronist unions were an important part of the government. Although the *Confederación General del Trabajo* (henceforth CGT) controlled the Ministry of Labour and with it a developed apparatus of control on grassroots organizations and local branches, they could not block worker mobilizations and the new forms of grassroots organization that started to emerge, the *coordinadoras*.

The military regime that took power in Argentina with the 1976 coup represented, with respect to previous authoritarian and repressive governments, a quantitative and qualitative change in the forms of repression and ways in which it was implemented. The military intervention was officially justified by the state of anarchy, insurrection and guerrilla action, by the necessity to recover from an acute economic crisis and by a general state of 'sickness' that the virus of subversion and corruption had provoked in the body of the nation (to paraphrase the generals). On the basis of this 'diagnosis', the military call for a Process of National Reorganisation was in reality not just planned with the idea of enforcing order in the country but rather with the aim of proceeding to a complete refoundation of the state and of society under the headings of discipline, Catholicism and the free market. Considering the scope of this operation, the elimination of resistance and rebellion had to be carried out in all spheres of society: at the workplace, in the universities, in the trade unions and in community associations, not just with regard to militant guerrilla organizations (Godio 2000).[11] The military *junta* was convinced that to stop waves of mobilization, strikes and the political power of the trade unions, decisive action had to be taken against the whole labour movement, both in its militant and independent forms and in the more centralized and bureaucratic union confederations. On the one hand, repression had to be exercised against the more militant, independent expressions of unionism of that time. The experience of *clasismo* and of anti-bureaucratic unionism was still fresh. This type of grassroots movement, fostering a democratic participation in union affairs and promoting the effective protection of workers' rights in the plants, was the first target for the military. In their words these unions were performing a subversive activity and had to be physically destroyed since they were considered a form of guerrilla, a workplace guerrilla *(guerrilla fabril)*. On the other hand, the central confederation could represent a channel for future mobilization and the centre of a political opposition to the dictatorship. The CGT, and the 62 Peronist Organisations that represented its backbone, were a threat to the military and the anti-labour project they wanted to implement, and were at the same time the symbol and reality of the power of the Labour Movement and Peronism. In the very first days of the coup the CGT and the major national union federations were put under direct government control, many leaders were arrested and military administrators were appointed to replace them. At the same time shop-floor delegates and internal commissions literally disappeared, were forbidden or made ineffective by both military takeover of local trade unions branches and companies' anti-union campaigns. In many cases the companies willingly participated in military repression, providing lists of activists and militants to the police forces, erasing entire shop-floor commissions, extending control over workers' private lives and increasing the pace of production. These actions transformed the plant into a jail in which the aim was to break all forms of resistance and opposition (Falcón 1982). Abós (1984) refers to the unlimited use of the police forces that were called in by companies to intimidate the workers and 'convince' them that protest was counterproductive and often too risky. In the absence of any form of protection, workers had little option then but to accept the rules and regulations imposed by their employers.

> When we consider the period 1976/1979 we have to take into consideration the terrible charge that was attached to each industrial conflict: the worker who challenged management authority, no matter if to a lesser or greater extent, could risk his employment at first and, quite frequently, his freedom, security, his own life [...] ideological persecution was also another constant of that period. The worker with a political or unionist

background was immediately labelled as subversive and this was sufficient justification not to employ him/her. (Author's translation from Spanish, Abós 1984, p. 44)[12]

From these examples we can say that, particularly during the first years of the military dictatorship, the scope and range of repression was very relevant. Anti-labour legislation, takeovers by the authorities of national trade unions, elimination of activists and shop-floor commissions, companies' tightened control of workers' private lives and intimidation were introduced and/or increased. At the same time, inflation was growing, real salaries were decreasing and the workforce was reduced in key industrial sectors of the economy (Gallittelli and Thompson 1982). As far as the workplace was concerned, the combination of company and military repression, the blacklisting of fellow workers, the physical disappearance of leaders,[13] and intimidatory practices were a daily experience and certainly contributed to creating a climate of fear within all the spheres of a strictly controlled society.

Evangelista (1998) argues that the last military rule destroyed the utopia of the social change that during the 1960s and 1970s was a common denominator of social protests in both Latin America, on the waves of the Cuban revolution of 1959, and in Europe with the rebellions of 1968/1969. In the words of the same author, the unleashed violence of the military dictatorship created:

> a reign of terror, a process of collective unmaking (that) destroyed the links between social subjects and their perceptions of a world with which they had already lost all proximity and familiarity. After an almost twenty years interval and in the ominous reality of the memory, the concentration camps established by the so-called Process of National Reorganisation thus constitute themselves [...] as the originating scene that always returns, like a ghost, to take hold of the present, and without which it is impossible to ponder Argentine culture in the years that followed the military dictatorship. (Evangelista 1998, p. XIX)

Is then the fear and terror produced by the military government a ghost that has affected the capacity for mobilization of the Argentine working class? Are the assumptions made by workers interviewed on the disruptive effects that the last dictatorship had on their mobilization and solidarity behaviour credible? The labour conflicts that exploded in workplaces during the first months of the military coup and at other stages during the dictatorship seem to weaken these assumptions (Pion-Berlin 1989; Pozzi 1988). Just to mention the automotive sector, on the day of the coup, Renault workers went on strike and during September and October 1976 other conflicts emerged at Ford, FIAT Palomar, Mercedes Benz and Deutz. Most of these mobilizations were spontaneous, not led by the official trade unions – which were most of the time in the hands of the military – or by elected internal commissions, and were often physically prevented by police and business repression (Falcón 1982). Despite all of these obstacles and the probability of new restrictions, these grassroots mobilizations took place and kept alive workers' opposition to the economic policies of the government, reconstituting or strengthening internal commissions and in this way establishing the basis for further confrontations. At a national level, the trade unions, after an initial period of disorganization, rebuilt their structures, became more and more confident in their challenges to the military and called for several national strikes that, even if not always effective, were proof of the labour movement's vitality (Abòs 1984).

If we look at the post-dictatorship period, 13 general strikes were called against the government of Alfonsín. In the 1990s again, other waves of mobilization affected the country, by both workers employed in the formal sector and the unemployed movement and marginalized groups, in these latter cases with new methods of struggle. It is, of course, unquestioned that these examples of mobilization occurred within different economic contexts, political conditions and organizational forms. The use of the strike during the Alfonsín *Unión Cívica Radical* (henceforth UCR) government, for instance, reveals how, particularly, Peronist unions struggled to keep both their prerogatives at the workplace and their political influence in the Peronist Movement. Alfonsín, as his party colleague President Illia had before him in 1963, looked at the democratization of the shop-floor as a way to break the link between trade unions and the Peronist Movement and facilitate his economic, anti-inflationary reforms (Roudil 1993). Soon after the government reached power, it aimed to 'dilute both the political and economic strength of the Peronist-dominated CGT' (Richards 1995, p. 58) and democratization in this context meant a process of 'de-peronisation' of the labour movement (Tedesco 1999). At the same time we cannot deny that within these political struggles the use of strikes was considered as an instrument of pressure by many Peronist unions in the CGT. They were mobilizing workers against the government in order to retain their power and oppose democratization but also to gain support for the Peronist candidate for the presidency. The CGT, during the period between 1989 and 1996, which corresponds to the first period of Menem's mandate and the beginning of the second, never called for a general strike, despite the workers' worsening situation. All this explains why, in 1992, the *Central de los Trabajadores Argentinos* (henceforth CTA) was formed, aggregating the unions that opposed labour flexibility and Menem's neo-liberalism, with one of its main aims being to extend its control of an increasing number of unemployed and marginalized workers.

Despite these differing economic and political contexts, it is undeniable that all these struggles had a base of support among workers and showed workers' disagreement with the power in charge and the socio-political model being implemented. But the fact that people mobilized independently of the nature of the party involved and the economic situation at the time shows the degree of labour conflict in Argentine society as a whole, as we will analyse further in the following paragraphs.

Despite this high level of conflict – both workers- and trade unions-led – there is evidence that the climate of fear and terror produced by the last military rule is, or at least has been, a reality for many workers and their lives.

As reported by Corradi (1987), O'Donnell and Galli conducted in Argentina in 1978–79, research based on interviews, life stories and testimonies, with the questions 'What does it mean to live under fear?' and 'What types of personal reconstructions can people produce?' The main conclusion of the authors was that there is a direct connection between the level of violence and repression at national level and the micro reality, such as the workplace. In these latter contexts cruelty, selfishness, depoliticization, lack of solidarity and individualism are the immediate consequences of a climate of fear produced by an authoritarian regime in the public sphere and by media dissemination. The public example is then reinforced by the micro despotism that can emerge in the various contexts of social life. All this creates, especially among the lower class, the condition for a state of political infancy and a search for political and charismatic leaders.

Noè Jitrik (1987) reaches similar conclusions in his analysis of Argentine culture. For this author the fact that repression has been mainly directed against political activists, workers and intellectuals,

> has also damaged the critical capacity of society as a whole, which, to the same degree, has been led to a form of cultural existence based on counter-values such as repression, self-censorship, vigilance, the acceptance of a subordinate and secondary scheme of values. (1987, p. 162)

In conclusion, from the discussion and the examples presented, there emerge arguments and counterarguments to the hypothesis that worker repression has acted as an obstacle to mobilization. There is evidence from the interviews and from the studies reported, that effectively the last military rule, more than other authoritarian experiences in Argentina's recent history and before the reintroduction of representative democracy, produced in many people a progressive distancing from political and social participation. This sort of apathy for collective action and the feeling of impotence could have been reinforced by the worsening economic situation, the increase in unemployment and a more general crisis in the values of representative democracy.

FIAT's and Renault's workers in the 1990s, if compared to the rest of Argentine workers, were certainly a privileged category. They were employed in a sector of profit-making companies at the forefront of technological innovation. Because of their position in the labour market, these workers had always been used to relatively stable jobs, good salaries and social protection in a context of increasing unemployment, labour flexibility and political corruption. Many of them, once forced to renounce any form of freedom in the climate of fear produced by the military dictatorship, could have found themselves unused to acting collectively or lacking confidence in their unions. We should add to this that they were probably disenchanted by the return of democracy. Indeed, workers' expectations of regaining their 1975 prot-agonist role in a context of more freedom and participation and, par-ticularly, their loyalty to the Peronist ideal of social justice faded away under Menem's neo-liberalism. This seems confirmed by the fact that, in the case of FIAT for instance, the *Unión Obrera Metalúrgica* (hence-forth UOM), the trade union historically representing FIAT's workers, had at the time of the conflict 200 members out of 1900 workers. In addition to this they were also working for enterprises that, in a con-text of disruption of any form of representation and of instability in the labour market, could have gained their loyalty. Job protection and retention of social status achieved became their primary concerns. At the same time, it is true that for young workers the example of the old and the lack of charismatic leaders, as well as the job stability and salary levels in both companies, were valid reasons for not engaging in collective action. If these conclusions are true, they nonetheless represent just part of the reality because otherwise we cannot explain why the same people mobilized in 1996. In the case of FIAT they occupied the plant after more then 20 years of collective inactivity, without an organization or a leader, and reached an unexpected level of consciousness and radicalization.

In conclusion it seems important to stress that the climate of fear produced by the last military rule, with its corollaries of apathy and asocial behaviour, has probably played an inhibitory role in the mobilization capacity of FIAT's and Renault's workers. But at the same time the fact that they did mobilize despite this heritage of fear requires us to examine and reflect on other factors that could have influenced the process of mobilization. In this section we have shown how workers have acted collectively – often in a spontan-eous, uncoordinated way – in defence of their interests, challenging unfavourable external conditions. These examples tell us a great deal about how the existence of structural conditions, set within the contradictions of the labour process and in the solidarity built into workplace cooperation, creates the necessary conditions for worker mobilization and thus of the need to start from this point in refram-ing a theory of collective action.

The next section will focus on the conflictual relations between the political, institutional and working class representative functions of the Argentine trade union movement, aiming to show the overall level and historical importance of grassroots forms of mobilization.

The relationship between workers and trade unions: political/bureaucratic leadership versus grassroots movements

The apathy over participation as a possible consequence of the last military dictatorship referred to above was primarily directed toward trade unions. In this sense the low union membership rate at the time of the conflict that we have previously mentioned might be an indicator, although not always a reliable one, of workers' opinions. However it is also important to note that the decrease in union membership rates and worker participation could be more a reaction to unchanging and corrupted leadership than to the organization itself. Bearing this distinction in mind helps us to understand why, as we will see in more detail in the next chapter, in the FIAT plant a previously nonunionized workforce voted massively for the election of a new representation and, on a wave of mobilization, subscribed in large numbers to a new trade union, Sindicato de Trabajadores Mecánicos de Ferreyra (henceforth SITRAMF). However, what field-work confirms is that, at least at the time of the conflict, the image workers had of trade unions, an image constructed from many years of working in the same plant, was not particularly positive. Workers' criticisms were not directed toward the role and function that a trade union should have as an institution created to defend their interests. The presence of someone representing them in front of the company was something natural, not just because they were really convinced of its defensive and protective role, but also because it was a sort of unchangeable and immutable element in their life at the workplace and, to a certain extent, in society. Trade unions in Argentina have historically played a pivotal political role that dates back to Perón's first presidential mandates. This represented a water-shed in the function and structure of trade unionism in Argentina and in the law and legal arrangements that regulate trade unions' actions in relation to their affiliates, the employers and the state. Argentine labour legislation recognizes the existence of one trade union per industrial sector and workers have no practical possibility of organizing themselves around a different form of representation. Workers can freely associate and organize themselves independently but they cannot take legal action, sign and negotiate collective bargaining, participate in arbitration or defend workers at the workplace without a legal authorization (*personería gremial*) from the Ministry of Labour. Due to the particular structure of trade unionism in Argentina, the legal recognition of a new union is always opposed by the historically legitimate union of the sector and is normally refused by the ministry.[14] This, among other factors, has in many cases produced an increase in unions' bureaucratization, a permanent leadership, extensive corruption and, often with the complicity of the company, the repression of any form of militant opposition.

It seems very useful to refer to what has emerged from the interviews as a starting point for further discussions. In sum this is what workers think of their trade unions:

- No democracy in internal union affairs; no participation.
- Union membership as a means for obtaining economic advantages (social security or social services).
- No efficient protection at the workplace; workers felt abandoned and tended to protect their own interests individually rather than collectively.
- When the union called for mobilization (national strikes, salary increases) this was accepted more as an obligation to the union and its delegates ('what will they think if I don't participate') than as a conscious act in defence of workers' interests.

These views raise a number of questions. Can these findings be generalized? Are they applicable to other contexts or are conditions specific to FIAT and Renault? Most importantly for this research, did the negative view workers had of their unions influence their capacity for action?

These questions play an important role, as they help us to focus on whether the historical developments of Argentine unionism could have had a more direct relationship with our cases of mobilization. In this section I will attempt to reach some conclusions on the basis of an historical analysis of certain particular characteristics of unionism in Argentina, by looking at how the structures and functions of unionism in Argentina have been shaped by relations with the state and how workers have perceived and questioned bureaucratic, institutionalized forms of unionism.

Trade unions and their relations with the state

From 1943 to 1955

In Argentina, for many years trade unionism and particularly a certain form of it have been associated, although mistakenly, with Peronism. Not all the unions were Peronist, not even during at his height, when the activities of non-aligned organizations were strictly controlled by government's authority (Torre 1988). But it is true that the majority of workers were genuinely Peronist and maintained their loyalty to Perón and Peronism to a certain extent until his death in July 1974.

Perón came to power in 1943 with responsibility for the National Labour Department in a cabinet formed by the military, which had taken power that same year. The project that he gradually implemented was a sort of economic Keynesianism, of state intervention, within a populist formula adapted to the specific reality of Argentina and to its capitalist development. At that time the country was still substantially an exporter of agricultural products with its few industries related to, and dependent on, this sector. The government, following a pattern of development common to other developing countries, fostered an economic model based on import-substitution, industrialization and infrastructure-building (Schvarzer 1996). This project went together with a rebuilding of class relations in which harmony and cooperation were considered essential conditions for national and common prosperity. Within this context, the state had to play a role of social mediation, fixing rules and setting agreements for redistribution of the national wealth.

The legal system introduced under Perón's governments facilitated the creation of a highly centralized and bureaucratic union structure. This system functioned within the state-directed and planned economy and served the political machine established by Peronism. Trade unions and trade union leaders, as organizers of a strongly unionized mass of workers and administrators of social security benefits, had a fundamental role. Within this framework each union, depending on its member numbers, represented a nucleus of political and economic power – often managed in the pursuit of personal interests and in an authoritarian way. The legal system that supported unions and so much empowered leaders was a direct reflection of the hegemonic political design of Perón, which was symbolized in the *'verticalismo'*, a top-down militaristic style of governance the same as Perón introduced in the government's relations with union leaders.

The powerful role that trade unions acquired during the Peronist regime was not just political/institutional but also effective in the workplace. On the one hand, unions often acted instrumentally, both mobilizing workers in support of the Peronist Movement and controlling waves of protest in order to gain political benefits. On the other, to maintain this political power and mobilizing capacity trade unions had to be strongly rooted in the workplace and support real improvements in working conditions and salaries. In this period, shop stewards organizations, the so called *comisiones internas*, increased their power and came to influence the labour process and the prerogative of capitalists in its control. Until the economic crisis of 1951/52, workers' demands could be controlled, but after that time Perón's efforts to reduce workers' power in the workplace encountered resistance. This situation of conflict produced stagnation in the economy and rendered evident the weaknesses of the social reformism promoted by Peronism. On one side, capitalists aimed to regain full control of the labour force and to increase their rate of profit by means of an increase in productivity and labour exploitation. On the other, workers and trade unions were resisting such attempts through pressure on the government, of which they were becoming the main supporter. The increase in productivity became the field of struggle in the following years between trade unions, local and foreign capital[15] and the dominant groups within and behind the state (Ghigliani and Flier 1999).

From 1955 to 1976

For more than 20 years, from 1955, when Perón was overthrown by another military coup, until 1976, when the last dictatorship came to power, civil and military governments alternated in Argentina. With the exception of the 1973–76 period, when Perón was re-elected to the presidency, trade unions have been the target of state reform and interventions that tended to reduce their financial, political and organizational power. On the one hand, with Perón in exile and Peronism proscribed for almost two decades, trade unions represented the active expression of workers' support for the movement and thus a barrier to any government in power. On the other, their shop-floor-based structures were an obstacle to capitalists' need to increase productivity and exercise control of the workplace. During these years the labour movement lost the struggle over productivity and was alternately defeated, repressed and rehabilitated but maintained a high level of mobilization and political pressure. Trade unions' financial power remained consistent as did their internal structure, their centralism and their bargaining power, despite various attempts to weaken their legal recognition (Godio 2000). This happened, for instance, during the Frondizi government (1958–62), which, in order to reduce the size of national unions in strategic sectors – like UOM in the automotive industry – gave the so-called *personería gremial* (as previously said, a legal recognition given by the Ministry of Labour and a necessary requirement for trade unions to defend of workers in courts, arbitrate or participate in collective bargaining) to plant unions, often sponsored by the enterprise. This was the case, for instance, of FIAT's Sindicato de Trabajadores de Materfer (henceforth SITRAM). Paradoxically, the independence of these unions from central organizations and thus their legitimacy in representing workers at the workplace was an important condition for the emergence of a revolutionary leadership in 1970–71.

A fundamental process that took place during the years 1955–76 was the progressive detachment of workers from the politics of the leadership. In the period from 1955 to approximately 1958, which corresponds to the so-called Resistencia Peronista (Peronist Resistance), with the central organizations under control of the military government and Perón in exile, the focus of resistance was the workplace. Here is where new leaders emerged in a struggle that, justified as a means for the return of Perón, was, more importantly, a struggle over increases in productivity and the control of the labour process. But after the big defeats of 1959–60, many of those who led the resistance, including UOM's secretary, Vandor, changed their position. They accepted the postponement of their claims for the return of Perón in exchange for formal state recognition and the legalisation of their organizations so as to establish the basis for autonomy in negotiating with the state and employers. The abandonment of issues related to the control of labour and its exchange for collective bargaining over wage increases were the corollaries of these agreements. In this new situation, after government recognition and with trade union leaderships open to compromise, workers' discontent could not find expression through their organizations, whose bureaucracy became further entrenched (James 1988).

Thus far, the analysis has been of how the function and structure of trade unions changed in its relation to the state during the first two Perón governments and in the period 1955–73. What we can extract from this is that in both historical periods the relations of trade unions and the labour movement with the power structures produced an increase in bureaucratization. In the first case this was related to the fact that the leaders were the repositories of loyalty to Perón and the workers were, in the main, loyal to him and to the leaders he nominated. But leaders were also responsible for the administration of substantive financial resources and this gave them tangible power. This point is very important for understanding the role of both bureaucratization and leadership within the Argentine system. Trade unions collected welfare funds at source, the so-called *Obras Sociales*, to deliver healthcare and social services and by providing this fundamental service they replaced the state, constructing citizenship around workers' rights (Martuccelli and Svampa 1997).

These political and financial reasons remain valid in the second case too. But when trade unions were antagonistic to power, bureaucratization was fostered by the government. The same government that, conscious of the mobilization capacity of the working class and in need of a legitimate interlocutor for negotiation, recognized the authority and power of the established trade unions. In a third case, that of the Peronist government of 1973–76, trade union leaderships participated in, and supported, the government, opposed independent unions, promoted intervention in local 'rebel' branches, strengthening their overall bureaucratic attitude. However, it is worth noting that such bureaucracy was not always monolithic or did it necessarily mean an incapacity or unwillingness to mobilize. Even during Isabel Perón's government, when the compromise of the CGT with the executive reached its peak, trade unions, pushed from the bottom (*coordinadoras*), mobilized massively in the national strikes of June 1975.

From 1976 to 2000

The last military government certainly reduced the role of the trade unions as political actors and introduced several reforms that attacked their financial power. However, the destruction of what remained of anti-bureaucratic experiences and the takeover by authorities of many organizations, strengthened bureaucracy. Internal opposition was banned and former bureaucrats, often in collusion with the military authorities, gained the control of those organizations still formally recognized by the government.[16]

With the return to democracy in 1983, the unions' internal democracy again came under discussion. The government of Alfonsín (Radical) suggested a law that, although maintaining one union per production sector, aimed to stimulate internal democracy and more transparent electoral processes, but the law was not approved because of CGT lobbying. In 1984 and 1985, elections were held in the majority of the unions, which were mostly still managed by the same leaders who had been elected before the military coup. More worker participation was allowed in these elections, in 70 per cent of cases more then one list was presented, pluralist fronts gained in many unions and this contributed to widening the political spectrum and internal democracy (Palomino 1985). But 90 per cent of the leaders elected were still part of the traditional Peronist unionism represented in all its variants (Fernández 1998). In 1986, the first CGT Congress held since 1975 lasted only two hours, with only one list presented and no further debates. It is significant how this culture of leadership, authority and top-down decisions that historically characterized Peronist unions was also part of a more general unionist culture, independent of ideological orientations (Godio 2000).

The permanence of the leadership and the lack of internal democracy were characteristics that remained in Argentine unionism during Menem's regime, too. Within the project of reconstructing the state under the economic and ideological umbrella of neo-liberalism, Menem promoted an attack on unions' financial and political power, while at the same time co-opting those unions that were more inclined to do so to enter the business of privatization of former state enterprises and to support the investment of social security funds in the market. Those union leaders who agreed to participate in these lucrative businesses then had another reason not to give room to possible challengers. Jozami (2000) argues that within a context of unemployment, policies against labour and a more general political apathy and demobilization, trade unions were forced to fall back on those bureaucratic and more undemocratic traits of their organizations as a means of institutional survival. But we will return to this issue in the next section when the socio-political situation during the 1990s, which directly refers to the time of the conflict, will be analysed in more detail.

General considerations

From this historical analysis, it is possible to say that bureaucratization acquired different forms and methods depending on the way trade unions structured their relations with the state and the dominant power within it. At the same time, cultural patterns of a certain epoch (for instance widespread use of corruption or intimidation) and personal characteristics of the leaders can make differences in the ways in which and for what ends a bureaucratic position is used. However this emphasis on bureaucracy does not mean that trade unions and their leaders have remained attached to a rather static and monolithic idea of their functions and actions. Contradictions often emerged between the base and the unions' top levels and in the labour movement as a whole, and we have to consider these variations while explaining the specificity of the Argentine case. Looking at these issues from a broader perspective, we can say that a process of more or less developed bureaucratization is certainly a general characteristic of modern trade unions as organizations set in capitalistic societies. The sociological school that refers to Weber has considered as inevitable a certain degree of conformity and bureaucratization, depending on the necessity for the union to become institutionalized. Marxists, as we have previously seen, although underlining the importance of workers' self-organization to overcome capitalism, have criticized the role of traditional unions as agencies of capitalist society and as performing not a revolutionary hegemonic function but rather a sectional or corporative one. These general interpretations applied to western unions are certainly also useful in the study of Argentine unionism. Nevertheless in this context, as discussed earlier, the same phenomenon has been shaped differently. According to Fernández (1998), the attempts to debilitate and alter the Peronist loyalties of the central confederation through legal reforms and repeated occupations of national unions by authorities under both military and civil governments until 1982 produced a need to identify continuity of action and unity of the movement with well-known and charismatic leaders. Moreover it was difficult to find workers who were educated and prepared to confront the challenges from the employers. This initial scarcity of competence was compensated for by natural charisma and leadership. Later on, with growing financial resources and political power, to be a unionist meant a career progression in the organization from plant, to provincial and eventually national delegate. In addition to this, the particular geography of Argentina, a big country with one-third of the population concentrated in Greater Buenos Aires, created a centralization of decision-making and financial resources in the capital and a relation of dependence between the provincial and the national federations, with union membership fees paid, very often, directly by the employer to the national or central federation of Buenos Aires. Another element that has certainly contributed to maintaining high levels of bureaucracy in the Argentine unions is their role as administrators and providers of social security services (Atzeni and Ghigliani 2009). During past decades, unions have managed a huge amount of funds, with which they have financed, primarily, health services but also all sorts of social activities and security plans for their members: from holiday hotels to pharmacies and from houses to pensions. Most importantly, in replacing the state in the provision of all these basic services, trade unions have acquired a central role in the daily lives of Argentines as workers and as citizens. This concentration of economic power, within a legal context that already favoured a top-down and anti-democratic practice in internal decision-making, added more strength to a perspective that saw the union and its leaders as performing a political and 'clientelistic', if not corrupt, function. As the cases of Renault and FIAT will show, in periods of enterprise crisis and massive layoffs, secret negotiations are often held between management representatives and union leaders in order to arrange the situation 'satisfactorily'. In these cases it has not been uncommon for the union to accept the company's plans in exchange for benefits and cash for individuals at the top of the organization. The rate of unemployment and the scarcity of social services offered by the state are today producing a renewed interest among workers in the services provided by the unions, which even if they are weakened in terms of members, legal status and political influence still maintain a relevant organizational dimension. This is, for instance, the case of McDonald's workers who, despite the anti-union practices globally adopted by the enterprise, affiliate to the sector's unión and its health cover institutions, so called *Obras Sociales*, for the social security package provided (Ghigliani 2005).

On the basis of all these considerations, it should not come as a surprise that the opinion many workers at FIAT and Renault had of the union was not positive. Instead of seeing the union as an organization that defends their rights against the employer and the state, they have, often, experienced a different reality: that of a centre of power, managed anti-democratically by a bunch of now-rich former workers. At best, if not suspicious they were certainly sceptical about if and how a union, at least like the one they had known, could defend their interests.

While bureaucratization certainly represents a salient element in the understanding of Argentine trade unions, opposition to such practices has also appeared cyclically. In Argentina, grassroots movements and workers' spontaneous protests (those forms of conflict that often go unnoticed in statistical reports) have repeatedly challenged both the leaders and the scope of their organizations. In certain circumstances these pressures from below became almost a constant of workplace relations and evidence those contradictions that Argentine unionism showed over time referred to above. The Resistencia Peronista (1955–57), the *coordinadoras* in 1975 and anti-bureaucratic struggles during the 1970s and 1990s remind us of those that occurred in other countries and at different times: shop stewards in the UK during the 1970s, *consigli di fabbrica* in Italy in 1968 and going back to 1920 or *comisiones obreras* in Spain during the last dictatorship. Trade unions are the institutions that historically have organized and represented those who work, but are not necessarily representative of all the different positions that can emerge from within the same class. In capitalism, the fact that unions tend to become institutions and set themselves within a system of other institutions (as the idea of a 'system of industrial relations' suggests) means that, in practice, they occupy an intermediate position, an institutional position, between the conflicting interests of capitalists, the state and workers, and this, in turn, can generate tensions and ideological struggles within the organizations themselves. This is the basis for understanding how workers have perceived and contested the forms their organizations have acquired at different historical moments. At the same time, these mobilizations against, or bypassing, the official union, often spontaneous in type, which have been recurrent in the history of the world labour movement, invite us to reframe our understanding of collective action. While not denying the importance of contingent, agency-based explanations (leaders, organizations, etc.), if we are trying to define the necessary conditions for action, our focus needs to be on the dynamics generated by the contradictions in the capitalist labour process.

Workers and the opposition to bureaucracy

In the previous sub-section particular emphasis has been put on the bureaucratic and contradictory character of trade unionism in Argentina, its different meanings and the reasons and historical contexts that could have explained it. But beside, and in opposition to this type of unionism, antagonistic, rank and file activism has often emerged within the labour movement.

We have mentioned earlier that rank and file activism emerged right after the military coup of 1955 during the so-called Resistencia Peronista. At that time, there was certainly a very deep sense of identification of unions and workers with Peronism. In the words of a worker:

> for us the return of Perón represented the return of dignity for workers, it meant to get free from the owner's authority, it was the return of happiness, it was the end of sadness and bitterness for millions of people, it was the end of persecution.[17] (James 1990, p. 128, author's translation from Spanish)

But, according to James, nostalgia for the golden age of Perón and what those times represented in terms of social justice and workers' legitimacy in society was just one aspect of a more complex and ambiguous sentiment. The unfavourable and repressive political climate also supported a process of renewed entrepreneurial authority on the shop-floor. Workers who once could intervene directly in matters concerning the patterns of production and the labour process now had to accept more exploitative conditions, less freedom and less respect. The harshness of such a situation and the daily fights on the production line and at a more political level contributed to the creation among workers of a sense of class identification that, while not assuming the form of an explicit class opposition, nonetheless produced, among the rank and file, a widespread state of tension. Workers genuinely supported the official Peronist ideology of social justice and class harmony and fought for Perón's return. But at the same time a more radicalized and alternative discourse started to emerge because of the inability of the Peronist ideology to provide workers with satisfactory solutions to their changed reality. This tension between formal ideology and elements of a class conflict produced a radicalization that remained nonetheless latent, at least during the first decade after Perón's exile. It was made politically visible in the substantially classless Peronist-AntiPeronist dichotomy. However it is worth mentioning that an ideological reformulation of Peronism within a more explicit Marxist framework started in the years following the 'Peronist Resistance'. These years corresponded to a confrontation in the Peronist movement between *'duros'*, supporters of an intransigent and revolutionary opposition to every non-Peronist government, and *'blandos'*, who were more open to dialogue and integration. In this latter group were the majority of unions that after proscription, in 1957, had elected new governing bodies openly in favour of immediate economic gains and organizational stability. Since the majority of unions were strategically oriented toward integration with the government in power, *blandos* soon became associated with bureaucrats and the anti-democratic, despotic, corrupt way of organizing and managing the union. The Marxist-inspired reformulation of Peronism certainly contributed to the questioning of, if not the entire capitalist system, at least the Peronist vision then of a society essentially based on class harmony and labour/capital cooperation (James 1990; Raimundo 2000).

Although the first signs of the emergence of an alternative rank and file unionism could be traced back to the decade between 1955 and 1966, it is with the military government of Onganía and in the newly industrialized areas of the country, particularly Córdoba and Rosario, that a more radical and ideologically mature unionism took shape. What later started to be called *clasismo* and *sindicalismo de liberación* was a class-conscious and revolutionary, at least in intent, movement that through the reaffirmation of workers' rights in the workplace, the control of the labour process and a system of democratic participation and transparency in the union's internal affairs aimed to establish a socialist state. In the words of Agustín Tosco, leader of the Luz y Fuerza union of Córdoba:

> the trade unionist has to fight with all his determination, with all his strength to change the system. The trade union leader has to know

that despite a 'good economy', if there is no justice in the distribution of wealth, exploitation continues. From this it follows that he has to fight for social freedom. The leader has to know that there will never be a good collective agreement within an economy dependent on monopolies. It follows that he has to fight for national liberation. (In James 1990, p. 307, author's translation from Spanish)[18]

From this perspective of national and social liberation the immediate aims for a union leader were to establish a direct relation with the rank and file, and gain the loyalty of the base through honesty, coherence, democracy and respect for different political opinions.

This approach to unionism, even if it did not conquer ideologically the majority of workers, who remained profoundly Peronist, was nonetheless accepted and demanded by the rank and file because at that time it represented a real instrument for the defence of workers' rights and dignity in the workplace and for their political participation in the society. As recognized by several authors (Brennan 1994; Gordillo 1999; Munck, Falcón and Gallittelli 1987), *clasismo* has to be seen as the result of a combination of factors related both to the specific situation of Córdoba, as well as that of similar recently industrialized areas in the interior of the country, and to the general political situation. In the case of Córdoba, the establishment of FIAT and IKA/ Renault in the second part of the 1950s led to the development of industrial activities based around the automotive sector and attracted to the city migrants from the interior of the province who tended to live in new neighbourhoods near the plants and share similar social environments. This new industrial workforce had no union experience, in part because they were young and had rural origins and in part because of the paternalistic policies adopted by the companies, including the use of yellow unions as in the case of FIAT. Events[19] of social mobilization and upheaval, such as the *Córdobazo,* united workers and students[20] in a demand for better economic conditions, in hostility against the patterns of exploitation in the workplace and in rebellion against a repressive dictatorship. The combination of these claims and the revolutionary potential of such a mobilization, even today still part of popular imagery, acted as a spark in the *clasista* transformation of SITRAC and SITRAM, FIAT's plant unions. These unions represented the prototype of the anti-bureaucratic and anti-dictatorial employee representation that effectively defended its members in the workplace through a democratic decision-making process. As recognized by Duval (2001), *clasismo* did not produce an anticapitalist position in the majority of workers in the labour movement of Córdoba. There was still a firm belief, incorporated in the Peronist ideology, that a better redistribution was possible. Nonetheless *clasismo* and the similar experiences of militant and combative unionism of those years were fundamental in the re-establishment, through the methods of internal democracy and transparency, of workers' control of the production process and of the dignity of workers in the face of despotic management practices. In the words of a FIAT/Materfer worker in these months of democratic unionism:

> in the plant, life changed completely. Shop stewards defended us with the foreman against all the problems that could emerge during work, we could control the rhythms of production that before were terrible. In general we could eliminate the oppressive climate that was normal in the plant and we could demand our rights as human beings. (In James 1990, p. 306, author's translation from Spanish)[21]

These anti-bureaucratic unions represented an important experience for the whole labour movement and a concrete threat to the establishment. This is best shown by the fact that, as we have mentioned before, the last military government detected explicitly in these forms of unionism a sort of guerrilla activity and devoted more attention to its eradication than to that of the political guerrillas. Trade union activists promoted the first strikes during the dictatorship and paid a high cost in terms of repression and disappearances.

If, during Alfonsín's government, traditional trade unions were very active in their mobilization, pursuing with these both the defence of workers and political support for the Peronist movement, during the 1990s their action was scattered, dispersed and, contributing to weakening workplace organizations, produced a further detachment of workers from trade unionism. This will be analysed in the next section.

The political economy and social conditions at the time of the conflict: workers' responses to neo-liberalism

The election of Menem in 1989 represents a watershed in many aspects. First it signalled the definitive supremacy of multilateral financial agencies (the IMF, World Bank and others included under the so called Washington consensus) over the state in determining the country's economic and social policies. Menem implemented a 'modernisation' process that was finalized by the retreat of the state from welfare provision, the privatization of public enterprises and the flexible use of labour. This was set within the neo-liberal policy of structural adjustment that was imposed by multilateral financial agencies on Third World Countries as a way of obtaining new credits. Second, the implementation of this programme required a redefinition of Argentine trade unionism in relation to the state and to Peronism. The ideology and politics of Peronism were part of a societal project that through the inclusion of labour and the co-opting of trade unions into the state aimed to achieve better social justice and the redistribution of wealth and development in a harmonious class relationship (this was concretely put forward in the period 1945–52 and unsuccessfully in 1952–55 and 1973–76). Menemism corresponded in the real world of the workers, even if it was not in the political discourse, to a radical departure from the idealized social justice in class harmony promoted by Peronism. In particular it broke the idea of development and redistribution with the state as a mediator and protector of workers. The Peronist ideology of the majority of Argentine trade unions was put into crisis by a system that while reducing their political and financial power was pushing them to adopt a business-oriented perspective. Third, the combination of neo-liberal policies and their negative consequences in terms of employment, the redefinition and internal conflicts of trade unions over their nature and their relations with the political power structures produced new labour struggles. These latter evidenced a new detachment of workers from traditional trade unions, the emergence in some cases of anti-bureaucratic organizations at a local level and the development of alternative trade union confederations.

In the expanding informal sector, the protests and resistance of the unemployed and underemployed led to a reformulation of labour-capital relations through new forms and new identities, *as* with the roadblocks and the movement of the unemployed, the so-called *piqueteros*. Social exclusion, exploitation and individualization in the workplace is what the working class (defined here in the broader sense of employed, unemployed and underemployed) has experienced in the last decades in Argentina within a financial and industrial system, now open to the global economy and highly dominated by transnational capital.

In this sense, we can say that the election of president Menem in 1989 marked a turning point in the Argentine political, social and economic scene. In the 1990s, following the neo-liberal doctrine promoted by the IMF, as a condition for obtaining new credits, the country undertook a process of profound structural change. This was put into practice mainly through privatization of public companies, fiscal bonuses to attract multinational investments, antiinflationary monetary policies, reduction in the number of public employees, cuts in public expenditure, privatization of social security services and labour flexibility. The Convertibility Plan introduced by Economy Minister Cavallo in 1991, fixing the peso/dollar parity, stopped hyperinflation and created stability and market confidence, providing the basis for a period of constant economic growth (during 1991–97 GDP increased at an annual average rate of 6.1 per cent) and political consensus. Privatization of state companies, due to government concessions and to the parity with the dollar, turned out to be a highly profitable business for local and foreign capital, resulting at the same time in extensive corruption, 'clientelism' and unfair practices, as in the case of Aerolíneas Argentinas (Thwaites Rey 1999).

But the euphoria of the economic stability of the first years of the Menem presidency did not correspond to better conditions for the employed and the unemployed. The official unemployment rate rose from 6 per cent in 1991 to 17.3 in 1996, while underemployment in the same years rose from 7.9 to 13.6 per cent (Lozano and Basualdo 2001). In 1996 the fact that neo-liberal policies were explicitly showing their weaknesses, not just in terms of social marginalization but also in terms of economic growth, was already clear to Argentine business representatives, too. In an interview reported by the national newspaper *Clarín* in September 1996, a representative of the UIA (*Unión Industrial Argentina*, Argentine Industrial Association) admitted that labour flexibility alone could not produce more employment and that it was a mistake to sell politically, as the government and the World Bank were doing, these reforms as the panacea for unemployment. At the same time he made clear that a broader social and political consensus was fundamental to implementing such reforms and avoiding social conflicts (*Clarín* 20 September 1996). Meanwhile FIAT's workers were occupying the plant and resisting, among the first in big industrial enterprises, the so-called labour flexibility. Once asked by a local newspaper for his opinion on the issue of flexibility, FIAT's elected workers' representative answered that he was still trying to understand if this: 'means that those who work are giving a small piece of employment to other unemployed or that what we are giving will never be recuperated and nothing will change?' (*La Voz del Interior*, 12 October 1996, author's translation from Spanish).[22] This process of reform was partly supported by the CGT, which at the beginning remained, despite internal divisions, politically loyal to Menem, a Peronist president. But soon the unions became the target of Menem's strategy because they could easily mobilize workers especially against his economic policies, which were producing social discontent. On the one hand, he tried to undermine unions' financial and organizational power and political centrality through an attack on their *Obras Sociales*, and a decentralization of collective bargaining. On the other, he invited unions to participate in the privatization of public companies and in the business of investing in the market funds collected for pensions and social services.

For the first time in Argentine history a Peronist president explicitly attacked the organization and structure of trade unionism, one of the pillars of the Peronist movement, and workers' rights. This action provoked an identity crisis within the movement and an increasing split between the central bureaucracy and the shop-floor delegates (Fernández 1997). On the one hand, trade unions were facing a direct attack on their autonomy and political power from a Peronist government that they had helped to support and put into power. On the other, labour reforms, consistently reducing workers' rights and benefits, were creating amongst ordinary workers a deep sense of dissatisfaction and anger against union bureaucrats and central confederations.

At the institutional level, the conflicting and contradictory relations between Menemism and traditional unionism generated a split in the CGT between those unions (or union leaders) supporting Menem's reforms and aiming to participate in the business created by the privatization of social security and those promoting opposition at both political and workplace levels. In 1992, the CTA was created mainly through the contributions of public workers' unions and former state-owned companies. This new confederation was thought of as a new experiment for unionism radically different from the traditional

Argentine model. In particular, the CTA aimed to unite both workers' and the unemployed's struggles that were emerging in different parts of the country, and promoted individual and not compulsory membership, independence from the state and the *Movimiento Justicialista* (Peronism), decentralization and debureaucratization. In 1994, resulting from another split in the CGT, the *Movimiento de los Trabajadores Argentinos* (henceforth MTA) was created with the aim of opposing labour reforms. After the creation of the CTA and the MTA, unions loyal to Menem and his reforms remained in the CGT. In July 1994 this group subscribed with the government and the entrepreneurs to a general agreement (Acuerdo Macro) that, while recognizing the CGT's financial autonomy and maintaining collective bargaining at central level, allowed the flexibility of labour, including reduction of labour rights, at workplace level. The last years of Menem's government showed a rebuilding of union opposition. The CGT, with support from the CTA and MTA, called four general strikes in an attempt to confront government intentions to decentralize collective bargaining. The success of these demonstrations, while saving the unions' prerogatives, did not change flexibility at workplace level, already recognized by the Acuerdo Macro and translated by the government into law. SMATA, the biggest union in the automotive sector and a supporter of the Acuerdo Macro, put flexibility into practice by signing several collective agreements with the big multinationals of the sector, including FIAT.

This fragmentation of unionism should not be a surprise since it confirms once more the multifaceted nature of unionism as an institutional and organizational form of workers' representation whose historical development always occurred within capitalist economies. The analysis of unionism as an expression of sectional and corporate interests, even if unions were representing the working class, was expressed by Gramsci at a time when socio-political conditions could have favoured the idea of an imminent revolution led by the trade union movement. In his words:

> Objectively the trade union is nothing other than a commercial company, of a purely capitalistic type, which aims to secure, in the interest of the proletariat, the maximum price for the commodity labour, and to establish a monopoly over this commodity in the national and international field. (Gramsci 1969, p. 502, author's translation from Italian)[23]

It is true that in Argentina during Menem's years in government, this natural character of the unions produced a perversion in the sense of 'financial stabilisation of the unions ... achieved by means of the legalisation of the instability of workers' lives' (Dinerstein 2001a, p. 122). This situation has been perceived in the workplace as a betrayal, one often symbolized by the contrast between the ascendancy and the material benefits achieved by certain union delegates, previously colleagues at work, and the unemployment or the worsened labour conditions the majority of workers were suffering. This perception of unions, their anti-democratic internal style and the bad reputation of certain organizations in the popular image contributed to a further distancing of workers from their representative organizations. In particular, for workers who were still keeping their jobs, the constant state of insecurity generated by labour flexibility led to individualism and to the impossibility of maintaining solidarity and collective action in the workplace (Battistini and Montes Cató 2000; Dinerstein 2001a).

However, in Argentina the decade of the 1990s featured the fragmentation of the trade union movement, an increased distancing from the workforce and high levels of conflict and resistance. In the privatized state companies, the processes of rationalization and the closure of sites created reductions in employment and strong opposition from the workforce, as in the cases of ENTEL, Aerolíneas Argentinas and Gas del Estado. When company restructuring affected industrial areas of the country historically dependent on, and specializing in, one productive sector (e.g. metallurgy, oil extraction or sugar cane plantations) resistance acquired a social character, and the defence of jobs mobilized different parts of civil society together: local unions, municipal governments and religious organizations, as in the case of ACINDAR's Villa Constitutión workers (Cangiano 1998). Although resistance encountered strong company and government repression, it was nonetheless a characteristic of the entire decade even with increasing scarcity of job opportunities and social marginalization.

These first experiences of mobilization mainly affected formal employment, and even if they extended throughout the country, they remained basically isolated from each other, not finding the momentum or the political stance to express themselves as a unity. Although these mobilizations achieved very limited results in the short term, we could argue that they represented a background for those forms of resistance (roadblocks, factory occupations, popular assemblies and alternative forms of solidarity) that were put into practice in Argentina at the same time as the 2001 crisis.

Conclusions

The chapter has explored several issues that could have affected the cases of mobilization that this research is considering. First, the effects of the last military dictatorship on workers' potential for collective action have been analysed. A two-sided perspective has been proposed. On the one hand, a 'culture of fear' was created, and a process of fragmentation and depolitization at the workplace could have emerged. On the other, these assumptions are contradicted by the waves of mobilization that occurred before, during and after the last dictatorship in the context of both military and civil governments. These arguments and counterarguments do not allow for generalizations: not all the workers have been affected by a 'culture of fear' and its consequences. In the cases of FIAT and Renault, the climate of fear produced particularly by the last military rule, with its corollaries of apathy and asocial behaviours, has probably played an inhibitory role in workers' capacity for mobilization. But at the same time, the fact that they did mobilize despite this heritage of fear and unfavourable external conditions further confirms how flawed and necessarily contingent reconstructions of collective action based on the identification of existing preconditions and/or on organizational resources are. However important these may be in facilitating and building a strategy for collective action, they are not sufficient to explain all the cases of direct, spontaneous mobilization that, particularly in the history of the Argentine labour movement, have frequently occurred.

These forms of spontaneous, direct action may on the one hand be related to employers' use of repressive practices and worsened labour conditions under authoritarian regimes, but on the other also have a direct relation with the Argentine trade unions' political role. In the second section we have thus looked at how trade unions' structure and function have been shaped by their relations with the state and how and why workers have reacted against the bureaucratic practices of their unions. Bureaucracy is certainly an element that emerges from the institutional process through which trade unions, as intermediaries in the labour market, always pass. But in the case of Argentina, together with this 'natural' element, the process of bureaucratization acquired very particular characteristics specific to the context. Legal arrangements that date back to the first Perón government, and to the role of trade unions in its political project, and have been maintained through the years promoted the lack of internal democracy, the centralization of decision-making and long-lasting leaderships. But in this context we have seen how workers have often defended their interests by direct, spontaneous mobilization outside the union channel, creating alternative, grassroots-based organizations.

Thus bureaucratization has to be seen not just as an obstacle to mobilization but also to what could have produced a more radical opposition and promoted a change. Workers' acceptance of a bureaucratized, non-democratic leadership is limited. Trade unions as intermediaries between capital and labour may alter and manipulate workers' demands but they need to be accountable to their members, especially when labour exploitation increases. Depending on the particular situation, collective action can consequently take a more or less organized and directed form.

The Argentine labour movement history is rich in examples that help to explain the complex relations existing between these different forms of workers' struggle. During the 1964 CGT *Plan de Lucha* (Plan of Struggle), a totally bureaucratized leadership could mobilize workers in the occupation of 11,000 plants, something that for its importance is comparable, for instance, with the Italian factory occupations of 1919–20 (first promoted and later suppressed by the major confederation CGL). During the Peronist Government of 1973–76, the CGT at the beginning tried to freeze workers' protests and to eliminate internal dissent but in the strike of June–July 1975 led mobilization and showed its potential as an organizer of massive worker demonstrations. This explains the military intervention eight months later and the violent repression that followed the coup, with the CGT and so many unions being taken over by the military and their leaders arrested. But in contrast to the militancy of 1975, from approximately 1989 to 1996 the bureaucracy first contained, but then was bypassed by, a general wave of mobilization that was emerging in the country.

Overall, the history of Argentina seems to tell us of a very active working class, prone to collective action. The workplace has been at different moments the centre of opposition to employers' policies, to government repression and to bureaucratic leadership. Workers have responded to different pressures in different ways, contesting both existing systems of representation and capital's rule.

In the 1990s, a new split between the rank and file and the leadership occurred within a context of more generalized resistance of the working class (employed, unemployed and underemployed) to neo-liberalism. Three elements have contributed to raising the level of social conflict and to a certain extent could have influenced the mobilizations that occurred in 1996 at FIAT and Renault. First, the pressure of multilateral financial agencies on the government became influential as never before on political decisions. Second, the economic reforms implemented under IMF auspices produced unemployment, underemployment, an increase of poverty and, with these, social unrest. Third, the trade unions' contradictory position relating to the government and its economic policies once more distanced ordinary workers from bureaucratic leaderships and opened the space for a new anti-bureaucratic stance. This economic context and the opposition to bureaucracy have certainly represented a fertile soil for mobilization because they offered to workers involved in industrial conflicts a base around which their demands could be formulated and solutions, eventually, provided. At the same time, examples of other mobilizations and the development of a sense of solidarity with the struggles of other groups could have offered both an example and a support. However, at least in the cases presented in this research, as will be more evident from the empirical analysis, these external conditions have not directly produced mobilization but have constituted the social background around which demands and conflict could be framed and a support for workers' radicalization and consciousness during mobilization constituted. This justifies further the search for explanations based on a micro level analysis.

A final important consideration concerns the level of radicalization of social conflict in Argentina. For an external observer, the study of Argentine social history is undoubtedly an exciting, although dramatic, experience. Class counter-opposition, economic crises, popular rebellions, military upheavals and charismatic leaders have all appeared in the last 60 years of Argentine history in a much more dramatic and spectacular way, especially compared to post-Second World War western Europe. Both police repression and popular rebellions can easily reach high levels of radicalization as was demonstrated, for instance, in December 2001. Repression is repression and rebellion is rebellion because no other alternatives are offered, because the system does not provide spaces for compromise or political agreement, and even less so for a better redistribution of wealth. In the societies of the rich world, social conflict might be less evident, without open forms of confrontation, more structured and regulated by systems of industrial relations, but it has certainly not disappeared. Inequalities are controlled and frozen, to a certain extent, by the intervention of the state. At the same time the lowest levels in many of these societies have been occupied by an increasing number of immigrants, who because of their illegal status or of their conditions of legality dependent on a formal 'job' do not easily mobilize.

In Argentina class polarization is very strong, with roughly half of the working population without any form of job or income protection. When not even basic services are provided and people are abandoned to the vagaries of the market, radicalization comes more spontaneously. The music is the same but in the case of Argentina it is heard at a much higher volume.

Overall what this historical chapter has briefly sketched is how, within the dialectics of labour-capital opposition, multiple factors can shape workers' collective action and the forms this can take. In Argentina's labour movement's recent history, unstructured and direct actions have regularly appeared, becoming a distinctive factor in the country's patterns of industrial conflict. The importance of these forms of conflict, which is one of the forms of resistance that belong to the tradition of the world working class, goes beyond their numerical relevance. What the study of the dynamics of these cases proves is how the necessary conditions for a general theory of collective action are deeply rooted in the structural conditions generated by the contradictions of the capitalist labour process. The next chapters aim to link this theoretical assumption to concrete cases of mobilization.

4
Injustice and Solidarity in the Dynamics of Collective Action

Introduction

In the theoretical chapter we identified in the contradictions of the capitalist labour process and the solidarity built into workplace cooperation the necessary conditions for collective action. This was important theoretically for two main reasons. First, it was a measure to go beyond contingent reconstructions that, while valid for enriching our understanding of the role of specific factors in the support of workers' collective action, were not able to offer generally applicable explanations. Second, it was a way to avoid theorization based on subjective concepts, such as injustice, that while relevant in a trade union, organizational perspective, are not consistent with a general theory of collective action and thus fundamentally contributed to capital mystification of social reality. But it was also important methodologically. On the one hand, assuming that the conditions necessary for worker mobilization are set within the totality of the tendencies and counter-tendencies produced by the capitalist system of production was a guarantee against methodological individualism. On the other, starting from this structural basis, we could have shown the logic behind the interconnectedness of different factors and how these are shaped by conflicting forces within the system, producing different outcomes in terms of collective action. Overall this calls for an analysis of the processes in the making rather than of static realities based on preconditions.

Against this background and as a first test of it, the previous chapter considered worker mobilization within the context of

Argentina in an historical perspective, with the aim of identifying specific patterns of action and their overall influence. Forms of workers' direct, spontaneous action have repeatedly emerged under very different conditions. These cases, in which no clear preconditions are identifiable, with no established leadership and in an organizational vacuum, most powerfully evidence the existence of the structural conditions necessary for worker mobilization.

The cases presented in this chapter, which occurred in the city of Córdoba, in Argentina during the period from September 1996 to May 1997, are further in-depth tests of the assumptions driving our investigation. In the first case we look in detail at the dynamics that produced workers' spontaneous occupation of FIAT's Ferreyra plant. In the second and by way of comparison we consider the trade union-led occupation of the CIADEA-Renault Santa Isabel plant. In the third case, which will be treated in the next chapter, we return to the FIAT Ferreyra plant to follow the events there, where a second occupation led by a newly organized trade union took place in January 1997 in a context of highly radicalized conflict.

The analysis of these cases does not intend to compare different models of mobilization, namely whether they are led by trade union or workers, or to express a preference for one or the other. The world working class has historically shown a wide repertoire of struggles and each is important as a learning process for workers. Having said this, the chapter does, however, emphasize the importance of cases of workers' direct, spontaneous action for the theoretical understanding of collective action. The study of the dynamics of these cases, in fact, puts into question the use of morally grounded, subjective concepts like that of injustice while at the same time revealing the existence of other necessary conditions for mobilization rooted in the structural contradictions of the capitalist labour process.

The chapter is organized as follows. The first part, introduced by the chronology of the conflict, describes the companies and the unions involved in the cases and looks for possible preconditions for mobilization. The second part compares workers' perceptions of injustice and the process of solidarity formation in the two cases.

The search for preconditions

The chronology of conflict

The research embraces a period of industrial conflict lasting approximately one year, from September 1996 to 1997, during which three factory occupations occurred, two at FIAT and one at CIADEA-Renault.

The FIAT Ferreyra industrial complex, historically the most important hub of the company's activities in Argentina, until 1994 hosted an engine factory employing almost 2000 workers. Following the decision of the company to increase its investment in Argentina, a new assembly plant was built in the same industrial area. This plant, a copy of the one existing in Melfi, in southern Italy, had to be at the forefront of technology and work organization, including a full set of 'flexible' employment practices. Due to the new production methods the company wanted to introduce (broadly speaking a lean production model that included *kaizen*, just-in-time and team working), a harmonization, in terms of working time and salaries, between the old engine factory and the new assembly factory had to be achieved. With this objective in mind, on 18 September 1996, workers employed in the engine plant were forced to sign an agreement in which they accepted the dismissal by CORMEC (the legal name of the engine plant owned by the FIAT group) and the new employment by FIAT AUTO, within the conditions of the new collective agreement subscribed to one year earlier by FIAT and SMATA, the biggest national union in the automotive sector. The day after the signing agreement the workers met again in the plant, discussed developments with their colleagues, realized that they were losing almost 50 per cent of their previous salaries and reacted spontaneously by occupying the plant.

After six days of occupation and with the risk that the case could become a nationally known example of worker mobilization against labour flexibility (on 26 September FIAT's workers were among the protagonists of local demonstrations organized as part of the national strike against Menem's labour reforms), the company, with the mediation of the local government, finally reached an agreement with its workers, who formally accepted a reduction of their salary of approximately 10 per cent.

In the following months, conflict remained simmering beneath the surface, with the company trying to oppose the formation of a new workers' representation by any means possible. In January, a moment of low production in Argentina, a new factory occupation occurred, this time provoked by the decision of the company to fire a workers' delegate on the basis of his low productivity rate. This mobilization was only partially successful, as the local labour authority settled the dispute in favour of the company, and signalled the decline of grassroots mobilization. Conflict did not disappear: there were acts of sabotage, disruption of production and partial strikes. But in the meantime the company was undermining the concrete bases for collective action, which forced the majority of workers to accept voluntary retirement and isolated the most militant workers.

In November 1996, probably on the wave of the events at FIAT, CIADEA-Renault's factory was occupied. Over two years the company had been implementing a programme to reduce its labour force. Workers were first suspended (but remained employed with a reduced salary) due to scarcity of production and later reinstated. In this process hundreds lost their jobs with union complicity. Groups of suspended workers mobilized against the company and challenged the union's leadership; opposing leaders emerged. This situation represents the background for the mobilization that occurred in November when the union, forced by internal opposition, decided to occupy the plant as a protest against the decision of the company to outsource the entire maintenance section to an external provider. After five days, an agreement was reached, but covert negotiations soon started that left things

Table 4.1 The chronology of conflict

Date	Event
September 1995	FIAT/SMATA collective agreement
18 September 1996	CORMEC's workers sign the new contract with FIAT AUTO
19–25 September 1996	First occupation of FIAT plant
26 September 1996	National general strike
18–24 November 1996	CIADEA-Renault factory occupied
16 January 1997	Creation of FIAT's independent union SITRAMF
22–25 January 1997	Second occupation of FIAT plant, activists are fired
18 May 1997	FIAT's workers' elected leader is fired.

unchanged. In the meantime the union's local internal opposition, although successful in the big factories, lost the internal elections and settled an agreement with the former leadership. Opposition ended in the CIADEA-Renault factory and with it any possibility of alliance among the automotive workers of the city (see Table 4.1 for the chronology of conflict).

The unions

In this chapter, discussions about trade unions are often associated with the words bureaucracy, bureaucrats or bureaucratic/anti-bureaucratic. This is partly related to the frequent use of these words by the workers I have interviewed and partly based on the historical development of trade unionism in Argentina detailed in the previous chapter. The word bureaucracy has in the workers' use a pejorative content and is associated with lack of internal democracy, distance from shop-floor demands and disloyalty. However, while these are historical characteristics of trade unionism and are confirmed by the analysis of the cases, I refer to bureaucracy only in so far as it is a factor contributing to explaining the workers' mobilization.

As previously mentioned, Argentine labour law regulated the issue of trade unions' representation through the recognition of one trade union for each industrial sector or economic activity. The Ministry of Labour is the only authority that can give the legal status of trade union to a free association of workers. People can associate freely but this is not a sufficient condition to defend their rights. In practice the legal system implies that even if a certain organization had achieved a high degree of representation among a group of workers, the power to act as legitimate defendant (in court, arbitration, collective bargaining and at the workplace) of the same group against an employer is dependent on a political decision. In fact the Ministry of Labour, through the recognition of the so called *personería gremial,* does not perform a purely administrative task since its decisions are normally lobbied on by the national trade union that has historically represented a certain category of workers. This regulation, which in practice denied the freedom of association, is part of the labour law system created by Perón. The aim was to support the institutionalization of trade unions, both tightening their activities and demands to the political objectives of Peronism and subordinating the unions' leadership to a personal loyalty to Perón himself.

The law that regulates trade union representation, the *Ley de Asociaciones Profesionales*, has been one of the most important pieces of legislation on the basis of which trade unions' political power has been alternately strengthened and weakened. Behind the decisions of the Ministry of Labour to recognize or deny the *personería gremial* there have often been national political struggles. This is the case with, for example, the Frondizi government's decision in 1958 to allow the creation of plant unions, for instance with FIAT's SITRAC and SITRAM and later Perkins's *Sindicato de Trabajadores de Perkins* (henceforth SITRAP), as a way of weakening the financial power and numerical strength of SMATA and UOM in the key automotive sector. But in other cases, government decisions have been targeted at balancing the power between two existing unions competing for the same category of workers. In new and potentially expanding industrial activities, particularly, trade union competition over the issue of representation in the sector has been fierce. Automotive production could not be easily and neatly classified since it included within the same factory many different activities and skills: from assembly to maintenance, from the work in the foundry and soldering to the construction of seats and internal instruments. When the first companies in the sector started to operate in the middle of the 1950s, two unions could potentially claim representation, SMATA and UOM. SMATA at that time was a very small union whose members were mainly employed in garages and mechanical repair shops. UOM was one of the most important and powerful unions within the CGT and represented workers in the metallurgical sector, who had increased in numbers as a consequence of the process of industrialization promoted, in particular, during Perón's decade. After the military putsch overthrew Perón in 1955, one of the first decisions of the new Minister of Labour was to recognize SMATA as the union representing the automotive sector, both as a way to undermine UOM financially and to curb its influence and capacity to mobilize automotive workers (at that time UOM was one of the leaders in the so-called Resistencia Peronista). In 1971, under the presidency of General Lanusse, the government decided, under pressure from the company, to derecognize the *personería gremial* of FIAT's SITRAC and SITRAM, since their *clasista* and anti-burcaucratic leadership were elements of social instability in the city of Córdoba and a national – and potentially dangerous – example of worker self-determination

(Duval 2001). In 1974, with union bureaucracy in the government, local *clasista* unions such as SMATA in Córdoba and UOM in Villa Constitutión, despite their high level of representation among the workers, were delegitimized and their executive committees replaced with delegates who were more 'in line' (Brennan 1994). After the last military dictatorship, the Alfonsín government tried to introduce more democracy within the unions, as we have mentioned above, but it did not challenge the monopoly each union had in its own 'historic' sector. Menem, despite his partial success in the reform of the labour law system, did not substantially touch the *Ley de Asociaciones Profesionales*. He needed the traditional unions' political power as a support for his anti-labour social economic reforms, and the introduction of more democracy in the workplace would have meant reducing the influence of union bureaucrats on the labour force, and with this increasing the chances of grassroots movements in opposition to the government's policies.

These historical examples are important to understanding worker representation at FIAT and CIADEA-Renault in 1996 during the mobilization that occurred in both plants. In the case of FIAT in particular, the historical antagonism between UOM and SMATA created a power vacuum in union representation that gave space to an anti-bureaucratic reaction. In the events following the first occupation of the plant, a new leadership was elected and was recognized by the workers as the only legitimate representative of their interests. After several attempts to obtain from SMATA legal recognition of the new representation as a local, independent section of the same union, workers voted massively for the constitution of an independent union, SITRAMF,[24] which was never legitimized by the government through the *personería gremial*. Based on this 'non-legitimacy' the union and its leaders were never accepted by the company, which, although forced to deal with workers' delegates in order to maintain discipline in the plant, never officially recognized the new entity.

After its experience with plant unions that transformed themselves in a few years from 'yellow' company unions to *clasista*, and with SMATA under a *clasista* leadership, in 1974 FIAT supported UOM's claims to be the workers' representative and until 1996 this latter union was the only legitimate one in FIAT's plants in Argentina. When the company planned to increase its investment in the country through the establishment of a new high technology plant, negotiations with

UOM started for a new collective agreement that would implement flexible working conditions in the labour process and concomitant reductions in salaries and benefits. An agreement was reached but the union general assembly decided not to ratify it. FIAT offered the same agreement to SMATA, which accepted, and became the legitimate partner of FIAT in one of the first flexible collective agreements in the industrial sector in Argentina. Similar agreements were signed in the same year by the same union with other automotive producers. It is important to recall that in 1995 when the agreement was signed, UOM was starting to oppose Menem's labour policies. Nonetheless, the union supported his presidential campaign during the same year, but soon after his re-election the same union started to lead a critical opposition to the government from within the CGT. In the country as a whole, a situation of social unrest was already emerging as a consequence of the privatization of state enterprises and an increase in unemployment and the precariousness of jobs. In this context, an internal CGT struggle started around the issue of flexibility. While the UOM opposition radicalized, SMATA openly favoured the introduction of flexible working agreements as it saw, with the arrival of new investment in the automotive sector and the potential of new jobs that the new plants would generate, the possibility of attaining a strategic role within the CGT.

Before 1996, when the new plant was inaugurated, FIAT's presence in Argentina consisted of an engine factory employing almost 2000 workers under a contract, signed with UOM in 1975 and updated over the following years, which in terms of benefits and salaries was considered among the best in the whole industrial sector. The new agreement signed by the company with SMATA was considerably worse than the previous one. The first obvious difference was in salaries, which were halved, together with a general reduction or suppression of other benefits and allowances: holidays, extra time, study leave and job categories. But most importantly, and less obviously, the new agreement also changed the working week reducing, as the result of a decision by the company, the normal working day and imposing extra time on Saturdays and Sundays to make up for lost time. Although this agreement was signed with the aim of implementing it in the new plant with a new labour force, the company, because of the *fabbrica integrata*[25] (integrated factory) production model, was clearly obliged to homogenize its workforce both in terms of salary conditions and production practices. This process was not easy since workers in CORMEC, the engine plant FIAT owned in Córdoba, had to be convinced to accept the unfavourable conditions included in the new collective agreement.

The change from CORMEC to FIAT AUTO is fundamental to understanding why workers mobilized, giving room for a new anti-bureaucratic representation. In the case of CIADEA-Renault, a change of contract, company name and union were not at stake and SMATA has always been in charge of workers in the CIADEA-Renault plants, co-opting anti-bureaucratic leaderships within the union's organizational structure. These factors did not give space for a further radicalization of conflict.

UOM and SMATA have often competed for the representation of workers in the automotive sector and for influence in the CGT, but interviews reveal that FIAT's and Renault's workers were not really interested in the way their unions were managing labour relations. This is particularly true for the case of FIAT, in which the workers' exclusive claim was for better wages. Opposition to the internal commission was dangerous since those who were critics or wanted to raise the need for different union strategies could easily be fired with company complicity. The foremen were used to teaching new workers how to behave in cases of trade union mobilization:

> '*Look, here people move in this way: if there is an assembly stay in the middle, don't be the first and don't be the last ... you are new ... and don't stay in the plant.' The same foremen told you to go and not to stay to maintain good relations with the union.*[26] (FIAT production worker)

Workers did not participate readily in solidarity strikes, people working at FIAT were considered as individualist and even within the plant there was a general apathy for all that was somehow related to '*hacer o meterse en el lío'.*[27]

This apathy for direct participation in union affairs could be related to many factors. As previously stated, the last military dictatorship could have played an important role in this sense. But it is also true that the way the union was managed, its complicity with the company and the impossibility of changing the leadership, even at plant level, discouraged workers from participating. In addition to this, a consistent group of them over the years became increasingly more interested in their own salaries and job stability than in collective issues. Many workers who participated in the creation of the anti-bureaucratic SITRAC went, after that democratic experience was repressed, through many years of bureaucratic unionism, military repression and market crises that consistently affected their non-participation. In summary we could consider all this as obvious evidence that before mobilization there was no solidarity but, as specified in the theoretical chapter, if we think of solidarity as a process there is no contradiction in considering it as the basis of collective action.

At the time of the conflict, in September 1996, there was a generally discredited view of the union in the plant and at national level. UOM represented the paradigmatic example of the orthodox Peronist union and its two contradictory positions, being both a national political actor as well as a counterpart to management in the workplace. Its permanent leader, Lorenzo Miguel, had been in charge of the union since 1970, and over all these years, he had changed his political position many times depending on which government was in charge and his influence in the labour movement. The FIAT workers' opinion on the trade union was also uniformly shared by Renault workers, as we can see from the following quotations: *'The union has been bought, it laid off more than the company'*; *'they seem lambs but are wolves'* (CIADEA-Renault maintenance worker); *'I could also tell you about the union but I don't know in what way this can be useful for you [...] we don't trust too much in the union, they are all bought off'*; *'the union on one side was defending us and on the other side was smashing our head'* (CIADEA-Renault production worker); *'the union is a conniver and permanently in power'*; *'is like the mafia, not more and not less'*; *'the same people that were in the union with the military continue in the leadership of the union, it is the mafia'* (CIADEA-Renault production worker).[28] In conclusion, it can be said that the combination of the legal system and the bureaucratic style of unionism contributed to creating among workers in both plants a discredited image of the unions. Together with these factors, the inheritance from the last military dictatorship and the fear of losing a comparatively well-paid job could have increased workers' apathy for participation in collective issues. Other factors have certainly contributed to mobilizing workers, too. If it is true that there was, at that time, a generalized apathy toward participation, the fact that a strong mobilization occurred, especially in the case of FIAT, invites us to look for other determining factors as part of the same process of collective action. Therefore, the next section is dedicated to an introduction to the companies, to look at the way their managements have historically established their relations with the workforce.

The companies

FIAT is the leading Italian industrial group, with its core business in car production. The same family has always owned the company and it represents a still successful model of early Italian industrial capitalism. Probably for these reasons FIAT directed its strategies to the global market later than other competitors and it has maintained a highly centralized and vertical chain of command and a rigorous managerial style. In the last decades FIAT's previously centralized structure, both in terms of production factories and decision-making processes, has shifted toward a more geographically decentralized and internally flexible organization. During the 1980s the company opened new highly technologically advanced factories in the south of Italy that could be considered as sorts of laboratories and as experiments in adapting Japanese practices and the related forms of work organization to the specific Italian reality (Camuffo and Volpato 1995). This process of innovation culminated in the 1990s with the Melfi plant, a new plant in the south of Italy, where technological innovation, flexibility, lean production, Japanese practices and a, consistently, new collective agreement, have been jointly implemented under the label of *fabbrica integrata* (integrated factory).

In this context of change, labour relations at FIAT seem to have moved, at least in the management rhetoric, from a conflictual to a more participative approach, at both national and local levels. The company has for decades followed anti- or non-union policies and this has certainly contributed to increasing conflict at plant level within a general political instability at national level. Over the years, the company has been, to some extent, more oriented toward participation and cooperation with unions.[29] But the economic and financial crisis that the company has recently suffered, and the need to reduce labour costs, has shifted labour relations once again toward forms of management unilateralism. Nonetheless in 2003 two Italian trade union federations (UILM and FIM) signed an agreement with the company and the government to soften job losses, while massive mobilizations opposed the company's plans in all the Italian factories. FIAT's readiness to recognize a more active role for unions and workers in the management of everyday life in the plant is debatable and this not just because economic crises and job losses often increase the distance of rhetoric from reality. Huge differences between greenfield and brownfield sites, and between Italian and foreign operations still exist (Bonazzi 1994; Meardi 2000; Rieser 1997).

FIAT is a company that has strong legacies from its past, its own 'genetic code' and its peculiar characteristics. This is particularly evident in the case of labour relations. In the history of the company, management/work force relations have followed four main patterns: paternalist in the 1950s, adversarial during the 1970s and part of the 1960s, management unilateralism in the 1980s, and in recent years somewhat more oriented toward cooperation with the unions. The strength of these historical models probably goes beyond their simple embeddedness in the company's culture or in some sort of 'country of origin effect'[30] (Almond and Ferner 2006) if it is true, as recognized by FIAT's top industrial relations manager, that they represent core competences of the company (Camuffo and Massone 2001). This logic allows FIAT and its labour relations specialists to use historical and Italian patterns of relations with organized labour, or a combination of them flexibly, within the particular local context of legislation and union strength. FIAT is a company that has adapted quickly to organizational, technological and geographical changes but one that constantly exploits labour relations codes of practice, prejudices, experiences and mentalities, in ways profoundly related to the history of the company and, to a certain extent, to Italian industrial labour history.

These specific characteristics of the company and its labour relations style seem to be confirmed in the Argentine case. FIAT established its presence in the country in 1954 by buying a state-owned tractor plant in Ferreyra, a suburb of Córdoba. The company gradually expanded its activities to the construction of industrial vehicles, cars and railway equipment until 1982, when, as a consequence of an economic crisis, it consistently reduced its investments in Argentina. In 1988 however, FIAT bought back its former engine plant in Ferreyra from Sevel, an Argentine business group that was producing

FIAT cars under a licence agreement. In 1994 the company started to build, with consistent financial support from local and national governments, a new highly automated plant to be integrated with the engine plant, in order to develop in Ferreyra and in South America its second production hub after Brazil. During all these years the company passed through different economic situations and market crises but it consistently maintained unchanged the paternalistic model of labour relations introduced since 1954.

In 1996, the pride of being part of the *familia* (FIAT family) was the company's leitmotif. This was echoed in the social events organized for the workers during Christmas and other important holidays, in the public speeches and in the football competitions between different production lines of the plant. The industrial relations director was the president of a foundation that provided workers' children with scholarships and awards for advancement in their studies and the company had permeated workers' lives to the point that the majority of people wore the FIAT *camiseta* (shirt). There was a broad sense of satisfaction among the workers with being employed by FIAT and the expectation of further growth, as the construction of new plant demonstrated, also contributed to this feeling. People in the CORMEC plant were empowered, new courses were provided and career opportunities were offered for those who wanted to be leaders in the new production processes the new plant had to introduce. Workers were profoundly involved by the discourse of the company and they felt themselves to be part of a powerful company within which they could develop professionally and socially. This 'ideological' work was put forward through the foremen and in the local television channels, but was also part of more explicit activities that professional psychologists carried out among workers. In the years that preceded the introduction of the new FIAT/SMATA contract, workers were paid to attend group and individual psychological sessions set up to convince them that whatever the salaries they were going to receive, they should be satisfied with the possibility of retaining employment in such a prestigious multinational company. There seems to be uniformity in the workers' opinions that, despite their suspicions about the psychologists, FIAT's ideological action was successful in building confidence in the future and the expectation of growth. On the one hand, workers had no other view of reality than that offered by the company especially within the context of a general apathy against participation. On the other, people at FIAT were living in an island of peace and prosperity in terms of both employment conditions and future expectations.

At FIAT we were enjoying the summer but it wasn't like this for the workers in the casting sector and people were not aware of this, like a person who stays on his own island [...] he doesn't bother about the rest of people. (FIAT worker formerly employed in the casting sector)[31]

Renault workers, compared with those of FIAT, in the years before the conflict were living under rather unsatisfactory conditions. The company changed its name to CIADEA and at the beginning of the 1990s ownership was acquired by national investors, who started a process of workforce reduction and outsourcing. In particular, the company adopted a strategy of outsourcing entire production sections or of ancillary services. The change of ownership produced a redefinition of the employment contract to less favourable terms with a consistent number of redundancies accompanying each phase of outsourcing. Due to the method used to reduce its personnel and the length of time this took, it is not easy to provide exact figures for CIADEA-Renault's restructuring. In addition to this it was company practice not to use layoffs, but suspensions. In these cases each employee received a salary whose value was inversely proportional to the time for which he/she was suspended. The mechanism was a bit perverse and solidarity breaking, because on the one hand it nurtured hopes and illusions of a future full re-employment, freezing conflict, while on the other the constant reduction in salaries and incentives from the company forced many workers to renounce their jobs 'voluntarily'. When in 1998, Renault again became the owner of the plant, the numbers people employed were now reduced by half and production was limited just to the assembly of vehicles whose parts were imported from Brazil.

Renault has a long-established presence in Córdoba that dates back to 1954. First as IKA (*Industrias Kaiser Argentina*) and then as Renault in 1967, the company represented the biggest industrial complex of the city both in terms of the number of workers employed and the size of vehicle production. In the plants the union has always been SMATA, and workers suspected a union/management pact for outsourcing activities and were not confident in the leadership. Despite the common opinion of both FIAT and CIADEA-Renault workers showed about the corruption of their unions' leaderships, in the latter case an anti-bureaucratic reaction to it and an oppositional stance internal to the union emerged before the conflict. The two companies were experiencing two different phases in the development of their industrial activities. FIAT was able to create expectations and promote enthusiasm among its workers for the prospective new plant, while CIADEA-Renault was clearly going in the direction of labour flexibility and workforce reduction.

In conclusion, the two cases of worker mobilization have to be seen as the result of two different situations in terms of the companies' labour flexibility policies. In the case of FIAT, management promoted a sense of worker identification with the company by the ideological action of raising expectations of personal growth and career development as a consequence of the new investment. These ideas were put forward through the use of psychological interventions within a managerial plan structured well in advance to convince workers to accept the unfavourable conditions of the new FIAT/ SMATA agreement. The success of this plan could be also attributed to worker apathy for participation in union affairs, the basis of which could be found in the inheritance from the military dictatorship, the corrupted and bureaucratic style of unionism and the impossibility of real and democratic unionism within the plant. In the case of Renault, the company's plans were evident well before the mobilization and there was no expectation of growth. These circumstances were evident to workers who reacted defensively, supporting an anti-bureaucratic opposition internal to SMATA. But what they thought of as a new authentically representative leadership to defend their rights against the company and to defeat the weak and compromised leadership turned out to be part of the same bureaucratic union system.

Paradoxically, as can be seen from Table 4.2, the preconditions seemed to be much more favourable for mobilization in the case of Renault, where the signs of company restructuring were already evident and a militant opposition had already emerged, rather than in the case of FIAT, a paternalistic company whose workforce was dominated by both apathy for collective action and a culture of individualism. However, from the way events developed, it seems clear

Table 4.2 Preconditions for mobilization

Company	Corporate strategy	Workers and collective issues	Workers and trade unions
FIAT	Company raises expectations	Apathy and individualism	Union passively accepted
Renault	Company is involved in a process of workforce reduction	Apathy and individualism but support for new grassroots leaders	Opposition to union leadership

that while certain preconditions may fertilize the soil for mobilization, these are not sufficient to create the critical mass necessary for action.

Searching for injustice

One of the merits of Kelly's mobilization theory is that it offers a conceptual framework for empirical analysis. In the theory the *condition sine qua non* for worker mobilization is a perceived sense of injustice. Consequently, once the empirical investigation started one of its main aims and working hypotheses was to search for injustice, by analysing the dynamics of collective action and worker motivation in the two cases. Was injustice the basis on which the workers mobilized? What meaning did they attach to the concept? The description of the events at FIAT that will follow in this section can be seen as the description of the empirical limitations of injustice and thus of the need to overcome this.

> *FIAT signs the new collective agreement with SMATA. We had a plant that had to pass to a new company with salary conditions inferior to the ones workers had before [...] it was very difficult.* (FIAT, former REPO)[32]

It was really very difficult to convince 2000 workers to accept a reduction in their salaries by 50 per cent and to be 'flexibilized'. This is especially true if we consider that the company had nurtured worker involvement and had produced expectations among them. What could be done if none of the workers signed the new agreement? FIAT could not lay off all these people without getting a bad image in the community and the risk of political pressure. The company was presenting itself in the media as the employer of 5000 new workers; FIAT signalled at that time, technology, innovation and welfare.

UOM's internal commission never informed workers of the company's plans detailing the salaries they were going to receive with the new contract and always stressed that although a reduction was coming, it was only a cut of approximately 10 per cent of their previous salaries. The day before the change to the new contract, union delegates invited workers to sign a paper in which they gave the authorization to negotiate with the company a reduction of no more than 10 per cent. The company used this paper as the proof of the workers' desire to be employed by the new company, FIAT Auto. In a note for the press of 18 September 1996, the day of the change to the new contract, the emphasis put was on its voluntary character and on the fact that the company valued and positively accepted workers' requests and that from that moment on an innovative project in the Argentine automotive industry would commence. But in reality the change to the new contract was compulsory, workers ignored the new conditions included in it and everything came as a surprise even to the day on which workers had to sign. *'The day of the change to the new contract was a secret, we surprised the whole factory, everyone'* (FIAT, former REPO).[33] At the end of each shift workers were called one by one into an office with two doors, one for entering and the other for exiting, and inside there were a lawyer, a representative from the personnel office (REPO) and two guards waiting. Two options were available: resign from CORMEC and accept the new flexible contract with FIAT or be laid off, in both cases with payment of legal compensation.[34] No time for reflection was allowed, the discussion with friends and colleagues at work was impossible and the workers who passed through the office were accompanied to the gate of the plant by the guards. Most people signed, convinced that something could be done in the days after, perhaps by talking with the union delegates and that signing with FIAT could give them time to become aware of what the labour market was offering. In the words of one worker, the day of the change to the new contract is described as follows:

> *One day you came in, they grabbed you, and the boss was telling you not to put the machine on and instead you had to go to talk with the*

REPO and he had your resignation and your new contract and you had to sign and a guard was standing beside him. If you wanted time to think about it, they did not allow it, you had either to stay or to leave. Many in that situation signed thinking that after they could change something and others did not accept from the beginning and gave up the job. If you go to your job that has always been the same and from one day to the next they tell you that you have to resign and that they will reduce your salary by 50% and that if you do not like it you are laid off [...] you start freezing, you do not have other perspectives, you do not even have the time to think about a different job or to invest your savings in something different. (FIAT worker)[35]

The day of the change to the new contract and the way it was implemented were the sparks for the mobilization that started next day. There were a number of factors associated with that compulsory signature, the combination of which produced the basis for mobilization. First there was a surprise: workers were convinced that the new contract did not imply any substantial reduction in the salary or a change in the working practices for them. Second they were feeling impotent and scared at the same time in relation to a decision that was against their interests and of which they did not know in advance. Third, these feelings transformed themselves into a search for those responsible for their condition: the company and the union.

We hated both the company and the union bureaucrats. The occupation was against the company but we also went to the delegate's houses, we wanted to beat them up and destroy their houses. All of them disappeared that night from Córdoba...usually it's the bureaucracy that scares us, that beats us, but in that case it was the opposite. (FIAT activist)[36]

The majority of workers were supporters of the company, they wore the FIAT *camiseta* and there were people with many years of working in the plant who were grateful to the company for what they had received over that time – the money representing just one aspect of the upward social mobility they acquired while employed by FIAT.

Yes, all of us were wearing it (the shirt). When I was ordered: 'do this or do that', I have always executed the order, I have always complied with the obligations of my work. We were very happy with the situation we were living in, we were interested in the productivity of the plant. (FIAT worker)[37]

Confidence in the union was compromised because of the opinion workers held on their union representatives. For the same reason, they were expecting improvements and job security from FIAT that the company had continuously stressed to them: they felt they were an essential part of a modernization process, of an industrial adventure where they were among the protagonists.

the company did not stress just aspects of production but also involved workers' families in the whole productive process in the big FIAT family. We celebrated birthdays for all the children, there were gifts for Christmas and New year, books, paper and stationery for the school, ... it was total involvement not just in production, it was ideological, for me it was terrible because I could see what in reality all this meant and I was feeling isolated. (FIAT activist)[38]

After the change to the new contract and in the nightly discussions with their families, workers were trying to define their feelings and to give an explanation to the situation in which they were living: '(the change of contract) *broke an entire life project, it destroyed myself and my family, I could not accept that idea*' (member of the independent union commission)

you were feeling as though someone had robbed you, it is like when you buy a toy for a kid and when you are going to give him, and the kid with all the expectations of playing with it, you tell him 'it was not for you it was for someone else'. (Independent union delegate)

In that plant people always worked a lot, production rhythms were very high. People worked a lot but they were proud to be employed by that company. They did not want to accept this and people felt betrayed, assaulted (injured). (FIAT's workers' elected representative)[39]

The reduction in salary was the most obvious change workers had to accept, but it was not the only reason and justification for their reactions. What they had earned was considered as an acknowledgement of their capacity for work and a sort of company respect for their human qualities. They could not tolerate thinking about a different life style, they could not accept the company's behaviour and they could not admit a limitation on what they saw as their legitimate rights: the labour-wage relationship was now unbalanced. *'We did not like the idea* (of the change of contract), *because we already had a living standard that we did not want to change, moreover, as it is for all people, we were aiming to have much more and not to go backwards'* (FIAT independent union delegate).

Wage reduction, associated as it was in this case to a change to a more flexible contract, may be perceived as unjust and sufficient to generate a mobilization. But in other contexts the reality is much more complex. As we will see in the case of CIADEA-Renault, the workers mobilized against the subcontracting of maintenance workers to another company with the same salary and working conditions. In this sense, was their definition and perception of injustice much 'milder' than that of FIAT's workers? If this is the case should we then consider that there are different levels of injustice? These questions certainly seem to go in the same direction as what was argued in the theoretical chapter about the subjective nature of injustice and the impossibility of considering it as a central element in a theory of mobilization. Injustice does not exist on its own, it does not have any objective dimension, but it is rather the result of individual perceptions framed within specific social and cultural models.

Problems in the analysis of data considering injustice as the basis of mobilization, appeared again in interviews with people who were still working in the FIAT plant and who experienced those moments of mobilization but without being actively involved. I approached those kinds of people who maintained the strongest affection for the company. They did not like the decision of the company to cut their salaries. It was painful, as they had to adapt to a different style of life. But notwithstanding this, individually they came to accept and justify the new labour conditions.

> *You have to be realist and always stay with the company. You have to be fully aware that a company pays a salary for the work that a person does and you have to agree with those working conditions. I have always been on that side, if I do not like it I will not stay. But if at that moment I was behind a machine, doing the same thing and earning less than*

before, I could not tell you what I could have done. (FIAT REPO, former production worker)[40]

Others stressed the view that their sacrifice was justified by the fact that young workers were now entering the plant and that was an important social development for the entire community. The majority of them accepted the agreement because of the responsibility they had for their families, they dared not even think if it was unjust to cut their salaries while a group of people was depending on them. *'I have a family, I cannot say "well, I give up the job" if there is no other option. The point is that I am not alone, depending on me there is a group of people. Unfortunately that's the way it is'* (FIAT worker).[41]

Generally it appeared that working in the plant was somehow 'addictive' for those people who had already spent a number of years in the factory, and this applied to both FIAT and Renault workers. The rhythms of the factory, a certain stability and social recognition over the years, the repetitiveness of a life structured around the plant, the development of inflexible skills adapted specifically to the production of car parts, created in many people, including those who initially mobilized, a dependency on the factory.

The point is that those people that have passed, in practice, a life inside the factory maybe do not see things as one who has thought to leave the factory. A person that lived inside there, when he goes from the plant to the street looking for a job, does not even know how to sell something. He structured his life working there and if you send him to the corner to sell a 'Mantecol', (popular biscuit frequently sold in street kiosks) he does not know how to do it. (Member of the independent union commission)[42]

In this sense we could say that working in the factory is in itself a mechanism that inhibits the possibility for mobilization and that could explain why people accept reductions of their rights/salaries. Despite the fact that individual workers may perceive a specific situation as unjust, their sense of injustice and their possible reactions tend to remain blocked by structural constraints (the need to keep their job because no alternative options are offered, the responsibilities of the family or the inadaptability to a working life outside the factory) and the impossibility to identify a collective agent.

On the day of the factory occupation, which also corresponded to the beginning of mobilization, the workers did not know what to do. They were of course feeling uncomfortable with the new situation. The union delegates had disappeared, for the company a normal day of work was starting, but there were no recognized leaders and no organization; nobody knew what to do. People started to work but only for a few hours.

> *The day after we entered the plant and we found a very strange situation. I entered a little bit later, the quality department entered later than others, and we had to pass through the plant, there was a very strange atmosphere there. People meeting together in all corners, everybody was meeting, it was as though the day could not start. We reached the changing room but we did not even change, 'a mate is saying that we have to gather'. And it was something spontaneous. We went forward to the small square in front of the plant, none of the union delegates was there, 'this is not what they had told us ... somebody should explain ... let's go to ask for explanations, let's go and demand some explanations'. And people went out of the plant in an orderly manner, I think everybody was there and they went walking forward, 'What is happening?'.* (FIAT worker, Quality Control Department)[43]

The factory occupation was spontaneous, unplanned and not organized. FIAT workers were not used to mobilizing and in the previous years they had just participated in a few national strikes because they were forced to by the union. People were used to solve working problems directly with the foreman and, individually, each of them had already accepted the conditions of the new contract. Even if the majority did not like it, nonetheless they had to accept it. It is just in the moment they met again at work that the mobilization started and with this their perceptions of injustice became explicit. Workers started to talk and became conscious of what was happening; solidarity emerged within the workplace and leaders unified individual sentiments. From individual rebellion and discussions among groups of workers the wave grew and people occupied the plant not knowing what they were doing, apart from the fact that they needed to understand what was happening. Somebody closed the fence of the factory gate violently and mobilization became occupation, at that moment,

> *we were lost, we had no direction, they had hit us very hard, so hard that we got crazy, we reached a moment in which we were not thinking, people did not want to believe, but it was very resolute.* (Member of the independent union commission)[44]

Workers felt violently attacked for many reasons. The reduction of their salaries was very large, the change to the new contract was compulsory, the company was responsible because it had created expectations among them and 'old' workers were particularly critical of FIAT because after so many years in the plant they should have received more respect. *'The "old" were maybe more militant because we perceived what was happening as unjust. After so many years of work we felt marginalized, and that we had no value anymore'* (FIAT 'old' worker).[45]

The internal union commission had worked against them, the delegates were considered traitors and there was no organization through which they could express their protests. They were feeling abandoned, their dignity as human beings was damaged, and by themselves and somehow they had to react, to hit back.

> *we went directly to fight and it wasn't. But they forced you because a different solution was not available, they forced you to fight. They made it (the change of contract) so compulsory and the salary reduction so drastic that it resulted in a very strong blow and you had to repay it with another strong blow, no alternative was left.* (FIAT worker)[46]

These conclusions became clear only when they met together and could talk of what they were feeling with the other colleagues. Injustice appeared in action, there became explicit.

The dynamics of mobilization at FIAT was very different from that at CIADEA-Renault and this was somehow connected with the violence of the blow received by the FIAT workers. In the words of one of them:

> *it was a terrible blow and in a very short time. Maybe if we were in the situation of Renault which was more gradual ... but in our case it*

wasn't. They broke us in the middle, they didn't dissolve us, they hit us directly and strongly and they broke us in the middle. (Delegate of the independent union)[47]

In the case of CIADEA-Renault, the mobilization and the factory occupation that occurred a few months after that of FIAT, have to be seen as parts of a process of company restructuring and worker protests that had started in June 1995. In that month, CIADEA-Renault (as said before, at that time the Renault plants were nominally in the hands of an Argentine investor) decided to suspend 2500 workers as a measure to reduce costs at a time of market crisis. Within one year the company gradually recalled the suspended workers but at the end of the process a large number of them had not been reinstated. It is in this period that among the suspended workers emerged a militant group who opposed the leadership of SMATA, who had been accused of supporting the interests of the company. This militant group won the union elections in the CIADEA-Renault and Volkswagen plants but was not successful in other workplaces. It nonetheless remained an active group with strong support, opposed to SMATA's permanent leadership in Córdoba.

Off the record discussions with many workers point to the fact that, after the events at FIAT, the SMATA Córdoba secretary – under the pressure of internal opposition – was forced to mobilize workers through a factory occupation as a way to oppose the company's decision to outsource the maintenance sector and to support workers' claims to remain employed by CIADEA-Renault. But after the occupation ended and the provincial ministry of labour intervened between the union and the company, an agreement was reached that in practice opened the doors for the outsourcing of the section.

In the case of FIAT, the mobilization was massively supported; it was not organized, anti-bureaucratic and opposed by the company, while in the case of CIADEA-Renault the majority of people interviewed reported the mobilization as a *joda* (a joke), something not to be taken seriously. Many workers were initially sincerely convinced about the reasons for their mobilization. All the union/grassroots leaders from other workplaces in conflict that joined and supported CIADEA-Renault's workers during the days of the occupation were of the same opinion. However, SMATA never allowed them to have an influence in what was happening at the plant and considered the case as an exclusively internal affair. But the way the factory occupation was managed by the union and the absence of real opposition by the company produced broad scepticism. In the opinion of one worker, the factory occupation turned to be *'a political/unionist agreement both of the union and the company that was in some ways arranged, in this sense we, the workers, always have to pay'* (CIADEA-Renault worker).[48]

The opinion CIADEA-Renault workers had of their union has been discussed above, and the occupation of the plant represented another indication of the bureaucratic style of SMATA Córdoba at the time of the conflict. Another worker, on the basis of his experience in the plant, identified the existence of a 'union thought or philosophy' *(pensamiento sindical)*, a sort of message circulating in the plant and referring to the way people had to relate with collective issues, in the following way:

> the union philosophy (the idea about the collective matters), was not to concern yourself with the problems of the others, 'you take care of your business and nothing more than this and forget about the others'. (CIADEA-Renault worker)[49]

Here again we can find the apathy and individualism that many CIADEA-Renault workers alluded to as a consequence of the last military dictatorship in their vision of the union. But this point of view was based on the style of SMATA, which even before the 1996 occupation acted as if it was CIADEA-Renault's business partner. Another worker:

> Many people say that in reality the union and the company arrange things among themselves but then say to people different things. It seems that it is like this because we didn't gain anything. We were feeling impotent and we couldn't even look for another different solution, with different people representing us because the union didn't allow us to do it. (CIADEA-Renault worker)[50]

In the case of CIADEA-Renault, the union bureaucracy was pushed to mobilize by the pressures of internal opposition; by the emergence of an anti-bureaucratic unionism at FIAT, whose workforce was legally represented by SMATA, and by a situation of generalized social unrest in the city and in the country. SMATA had to show a certain degree of militancy if it wanted to avoid the risk of being bypassed by the rank and file and this could explain why mobilization was provoked. We have seen how union bureaucracy in Argentina has often acted in such a way, trying to ride the wave of mobilization and taking advantage of workers' protests to win support for its actions.

In the case of CIADEA-Renault, workers were aggrieved by the company's policies but first scepticism and then reality showed that a mobilization led by a bureaucratic union was not possible. The sense of injustice did not become explicit. Injustice meant the acceptance of an unchangeable situation and transformed itself into impotence, frustration: *'we were all aware, all ... unfortunately how many "broncas" (anger, regrets, sorrow) we had to accept? Thousands and thousands of "broncas". You have to resist and accept it for the family, you have to tolerate many things'* (CIADEA-Renault worker).[51]

Developing solidarity

'Solidarity always exists, it is spontaneous. What happens is that repression, today the flexibility of labour and yesterday the army, and insufficient organization breaks it up' (SITRAC's activist).[52] This provocative declaration from one of the leaders of the 1970–71 *clasista* experience at FIAT, can be considered as a good starting point for the analysis for the following reasons. First, it offers a controversial vision based on two opposed extremes: the spontaneity of solidarity and an almost natural intervention of repressive factors. Second, the alternation of these two extremes and the various situations that can emerge in between introduce a dynamic view of solidarity. Third, it also focuses our attention on repressive conditions external to the workplace (labour flexibility and the army). Fourth, it gives importance in strengthening solidarity to aspects related to organization and leadership, thus linking structural conditions to agency factors. Is solidarity always spontaneous? What does spontaneity mean in the workplace context? Can we measure the level of solidarity? What is the relationship between spontaneous solidarity and leadership/organization?

The cases of FIAT and Renault help to answer some of these questions and define more clearly the importance of solidarity within collective action. Central to this is the method we use to analyse

solidarity. Solidarity is a process, not a static reality. Empirical analyses can show contradictory results if extrapolated from a context
dominated by a system-imposed tendency and counter-tendencies.
On the one hand there may be cases in which solidarity does not
explicitly appear as the result of the combined action of different
factors: a company's industrial relations approach, stagnation of the
labour market, a bureaucratic union's control of the workforce or
an unfavourable economic and political situation. Factors like these
could be the cause of the ineffectiveness/limitation of the action of
solidarity, giving the impression that, in certain workplaces, there is
no solidarity at all. On the other hand, there could be situations in
which the existence of active solidarity among a group of workers
is overestimated despite evidence of its pre-existence. Mobilizations
do not always achieve what unions expect, while conversely workers
can show unexpected levels of cohesion and be able to organize a
protest. On the basis of the above considerations, looking at solidarity as something whose pre-existence has to be somehow proven
does not help us to understand its role in a case of collective action.
The point we should stress is that of the dynamic nature of solidarity, following the argument presented in the theoretical chapter; we
have to analyse it as a process originated and built in the cooperation
of the labour process, but whose formation can be influenced differently by internal and external factors. Following this, this section
will focus on the various moments that have constituted the process
of the formation of solidarity.

The issue of solidarity appeared most explicitly in the interviews
with FIAT workers. If in this case workers have experienced a sort
of 'progressive', 'increasing' sense of the strength of their solidarity, Renault workers have, in contrast, experienced a 'regression'.
This negative perception has profoundly influenced their accounts,
which as a result appear less intense and full of scepticism, although
no less interesting, than those of FIAT workers.

In the case of FIAT we have a heterogeneous group of workers.
At the time of conflict the workforce could be divided into three
main – equally represented – groups. The first one included those
people who entered the company between 1970 and 1976. In the
second were those in the middle of their careers, who already had 15
years of experience. The last group was represented by workers with
just few years of employment. These workers, in the 20 years before

the conflict, never had a confrontation with the company and were proud of the quality of their job. They identified with the company, and were part of a workers' aristocracy who already had a place in society and future plans for a social and professional advancement:

> *People were not so much concerned with solidarity ... nobody wanted to lose anything because we had, compared with workers nationally, a good salary and a comfortable position. Those people that were involved in this history, put themselves ... didn't see that they were losing some common interests.* (FIAT worker, Quality Control Department)[53]

For a worker who had entered the plant in 1992: *'At CORMEC there were no reasons for conflict and not even union politics, the assemblies that we did were for stupid things, we sat there to smoke a joint'* (FIAT worker).[54]

In the plant it was even difficult to organize a small protest for better food in the cafeteria and active solidarity did not emerge because workers had no significant complaints about the company. They were well paid, production in 1993–94 was high and the company had no interest in provoking conflict. The plan to open a new assembly factory was creating even more expectations.

> *there was a high production level, we had to work extra time, the company needed workers because it was a moment of high demand in the automobile production in Argentina. There was a continuous and strong growth and exports to Brazil. This meant that workers were working on three shifts to satisfy that demand. There was no pressure from the company, they rather always tried to respect the rules of the collective agreement that we had at that time.* (FIAT activist)[55]

As a reflection of this, among workers there was *compañerismo.* The need to cooperate in the production process and the search for each other support helped to create friendly relations with the majority of colleagues at work, friendship with some of them and sharing of common social activities outside the factory. But this form of inactivated solidarity never gave space for collective action. *'at that time everything was quiet, we were earning very well and the rest was not important. Among us there was compañerismo, there were always parties, there were always people for this but not for the struggle'* (FIAT activist).[56]

The composition of the workforce was also a matter of division among workers. A consistent number of them had passed through periods of rebellion with SITRAC, repression by the military government and economic instability. This group in particular was a bit sceptical, tired after many years of confrontation and much more oriented to the satisfaction of personal and individual goals than to collective achievements. These people, in particular, after the 1970s were:

> *a bit tired and at the end we didn't see the objectives that we had as workers. Everything was done or could be obtained. In 1983 people were entering a time of democracy and freedom, we were at that time in a moment of transition. There were not too many things to fight for.* (FIAT worker, Quality Control Department)[57]

In the case of CIADEA-Renault, too, *compañerismo* was widespread in the plant and the composition of the labour force was similar. The union was more approved of than at FIAT and this was true at least at the beginning for some of the plant delegates; initial opposition to the SMATA Córdoba leadership was from a CIADEA-Renault delegate. Nevertheless, the general opinion was that of the *no te metás, haces lo tuyo* (do not get yourself into trouble, mind your own business). As previously seen, this was the 'old' attitude over collective matters and new workers had no other option than to follow that way: '*Those who recently entered the factory didn't have any examples because the only thing that they found was a lot of people nodding their heads and saying sì señor, sì señor*' (CIADEA-Renault worker).[58] But a difference from FIAT was that the company managed to generate a sense of competition and division among the workers. As we have seen in the section analysing the companies, this division was achieved particularly through the use of outsourcing and/or with targeted suspensions from work of groups of workers for indefinite periods.

> *The politics of the company has always been to divide us if they suspected that we would gather and build solidarity amongst us. They tried to create conflict and divisions among us ... I tell you once again, the one who loses is always the worker, I do not know if because of our lack of activity or because of their plans.* (CIADEA-Renault worker)[59]

'*The company contributes to the break in solidarity, I think. This was or it is what the company normally does, to break unity among colleagues, we lived all this down there, I'm sure*' (CIADEA-Renault worker).[60] In summary, solidarity was present at FIAT and Renault only in the form of *compañerismo*, people helping each other in daily production activities, but workers tended to look first to their own business and collective protests were the last issues in their discussions. If we conceptualize solidarity in a static way we have to accept that it did not pre-exist before the conflict and that individualism was, to a certain extent, the dominant attitude in the plants. Thus we might think that the mobilizations occurred as the result of leadership's persuasive action (giving credibility to the fact that an individual may gain over diffused individualism). This is at least what seems to emerge through an analysis of the newspaper articles covering the events at FIAT. In these, some attempts are made to outline the possible causes of the conflict (bad communications, the unions' internal struggles), but an extended part is dedicated to the workers' elected leader, his political affiliation, his life style and his acquaintances. Even in informal conversations the period of the conflict is identified with the name of the person the workers elected as their representative: *el tema de Gallo, la cuestion de Gallo* (the issue, the theme of Gallo). It is not in doubt that leadership is important for mobilization and that leaders are fundamental in strengthening it, but in our case collective action started spontaneously as people gathered in solidarity to discuss and to try to solve common problems. Leadership emerged after mobilization, not before.

Thus the question remains: how could a group of workers who for years lived within an individualistic environment have generated, between one day and the next, a solidarity movement? Is it credible that just in one night they could have passed from being *corderos* (lambs) to *lobos* (wolves)? But the opposite is the case with Renault, despite the negative culture about collective issues (*el pensamiento sindical*) an opposition and a leadership emerged; internal conditions may have favoured mobilization but conflict did not reach the same level as at FIAT and soon after the factory occupation ended, worker activism dissolved.

In search for answers, we could first look at the external conditions that could have favoured solidarity. In September 1996, when CORMEC was occupied, there existed in Argentina a situation of social mobilization, although not articulated and fragmented, and opposition to the neo-liberal policies of the government coming from both the organized side of the labour movement (traditional unions in the CGT and alternative central confederations CTA and MTA) and the early actions of the unemployed movement. Unemployment was around 20 per cent nationally, and in certain deindustrialized areas social conflict was becoming unsustainable. But if we think that this situation could have transformed workers' individualistic attitudes and strengthened solidarity links we are probably wrong. In the case of FIAT we have seen how the mobilization was spontaneous and not externally directed or motivated; workers did not know in advance precisely about the day of the change to the new contract and the scale of the salary reduction. They were 'like on an island enjoying summer', to use the expression of one of the interviewees. The fact that FIAT had decided to increase its investment with the construction of the new plant was another sign of confidence in the future and independent of what was happening in the country. Of course not all the people were unaware of the world outside the factory and none of them had a low level of education or an absolute apathy for politics, but discussions at the workplace were limited to a few arguments related to production and working conditions. The fact that the union, generally a channel for the exchange of information with the outside world, was discredited among the workers increased their isolation and many people in a certain sense wanted to maintain this. In addition, the high level of unemployment, an important external condition at that time, should have invited a fierce and individualistic defence of the workers' jobs and not a mobilization. As previously observed, due to the existing preconditions, we may have expected mobilization at CIADEA-Renault and not at FIAT. But despite the workers' identification of a collective agent, a mix of structural determinants had hampered the possibility of workers' solidarity being expressed through collective action.

On the contrary, in the case of the FIAT mobilization, taking advantage of the free space that the change of contract produced, a solidarity movement explicitly emerged, born out of a situation specific to the plant. In the 25 years before the occupation,

there was compañerismo and nothing else. That is why on the day of the factory occupation people were crying...I was crying, every half an hour I was crying. It was a situation for crying because solidarity, everything was unexpected, it was like something was set free, was released and this was positive for the people. It was positive not just in the economic sense but also as a way to feel realized as a person. They were feeling worthy persons and today everybody remembers that struggle and that they did well, well because they were feeling well. (FIAT's workers' elected representative)[61]

What happened with the change to the new contract affected the majority of workers. The reduction in salaries was the most evident factor, but a combination of many others contributed to create the particular situation that represented the spark for the mobilization.

it wasn't just a salary reduction, it was compulsory, it was an agreement among all: governments, trade unions, company, all together...at that time, I tell you what it was for me, I felt and even today I feel ashamed to have to say to my family that I cannot have the possibility of supporting them. I was passing from a certain salary to earn half of it and with many conditions of slavery and without having moved a finger.... I believe that each of us can react very, very violently when you are touched in something that you love more than yourself and if no other possibility is left. (FIAT maintenance worker)[62]

Many people at FIAT felt completely abandoned not just because the union did not act as it promised to do but also because of the actions of the company to which they had dedicated their entire working lives. *'I felt deceived and in that moment the relation that I had with the company broke down'* (FIAT quality worker 3);[63] *'People felt betrayed by the union and abandoned and cheated by the company'* (CPI FIAT).[64]

The combination of all these factors was a shock for the workers. When they had the opportunity to get together, they gave expression to their feelings, knowing that the others could understand and give them support. Solidarity was emerging spontaneously even among a group of people not used to conflict because there was no longer basis for individualism. The paternalistic style used for decades by the company to control the labour force, the 'golden splendour' of their isolation from the rest of the working class, disappeared between one day and the next. In this new situation, without those elements that had kept these workers outside conflict for decades, solidarity became the basis of their strength. In that moment people started to achieve a deeper consciousness of their position within the more general social unrest of the country and this contributed to the radicalization of their fights. As a worker bitterly summed it up:

> *you were living like a chicken for the slaughter house: you went to work, you ate from your little plate, you got fat and then you finished on the barbecue. It was like this. Later on, they showed you that they were going to make your cage smaller, that they were going to give you less water and food but in any case you had to go to the slaughter house.* (FIAT activist)[65]

In the case of FIAT, those factors that for years had kept the plant free of conflict and had made solidarity unnecessary, changed from one day to the next and were all summed up by the new contract. Identification with the company became disaffection and union delegates emerged as traitors. But workers reacted by spontaneously gathering and discussing, overcoming the barriers of individualism and activating solidarity, discovering in it the necessary condition for mobilization.

The case of CIADEA-Renault is similar to FIAT with respect to workers' individualistic attitudes and the discredited image they had of the union. In the interviews no sense of strong identification with the company appears, because it was clearly moving toward a reduction in costs and the number of employees, well before the mobilization. As we have seen, the outsourcing of the maintenance sector had been preceded by massive suspensions and selective reinstatement of some of those suspended. CIADEA-Renault never, and especially after FIAT's workers mobilized in September, implemented changes in the labour conditions or cut costs of its labour force so drastically and without a negotiated agreement with the union bureaucracy.

> *Here the company doesn't lay off, they suspend you, they drown you, they drown you until you say 'well here they are choking me'. But they never laid off anybody, they suspend you. They don't have to hurry, the one who has to hurry up is you because you have bills to pay and you cannot.* (Renault worker)[66]

Hidden negotiations between the company and the union's bureaucracy resolved the conflict 'positively'. Officially, the factory occupation was justified by the fact that the company wanted to transfer all its maintenance workers to an external company, Polymont, with the guarantee of salaries and labour conditions. Workers supported the mobilization promoted by the union because they saw the decision of the company as a first step to the outsourcing of the entire plant. But a few weeks after the end of the occupation, the union agreed a plan with the company that, dividing workers and breaking their solidarity, opened the doors for flexible working conditions and for a reduction in the number of employees. The dilution of conflict is one of the factors that have to be taken into consideration in the understanding of solidarity and mobilization at CIADEA-Renault. Workers did not face a drastic and generalized reduction in their salaries, flexibility was implemented gradually and competition among workers was fierce because of the real possibility of being suspended and never being re-employed again.

Solidarity did not reach the level of collective action because of a clear strategy on the part of the company to dilute the conflict with the active support of the union bureaucracy. This happened not just through secret negotiations with the management but also through the co-opting of the former internal opposition at the top of the organization. With the company subtly reducing labour costs and with no alternative for a more efficient and honest union representation, no solidarity could emerge.

> *You were surrounded with no possibility to move, you had to stay in the middle. Everybody felt fear, fear to lose the job, fear of the government, fear of the company, fear of the union. Fear, fear, fear, and the 'elders' that were there could arrange with the company and ciao.* (Renault worker)[67]

Conclusions

What are the insights that come from the empirical analyses of the two cases of mobilization?

First, the analysis of the dynamics of mobilization demonstrates the inadequacy of injustice as the central tenet in a generally applicable theory of collective action. Injustice is not the basis around which a mobilization can be produced, it is rather a subjective perception that varies when considering the specific case and the moral/ethical values of certain epochs. The comparison provides various examples of how injustice can be perceived differently, even within the same plant, as for instance in the case of those FIAT workers who remained loyal to the company. After the failure of the factory occupation and with the impossibility of changing their situation, CIADEA-Renault's workers were certainly uncomfortable and feeling their situation as unjust. But mobilization did not occur.

Second, the cases show how different conditions act upon the process of the formation of solidarity, reducing or increasing the possibility for its full development. The combination of specific circumstances in some cases may, and in others may not, allow solidarity to become active. We have seen that in the case of FIAT, with the change of contract, there was a mixture of surprise, betrayal and shock that broke the 'golden splendour' in which workers had been living and brought them back to harsh reality. In this context, without support from either the company or the union, solidarity emerged spontaneously, developing from the *compañerismo* built into the workers' cooperation to become the only resource available to them in defence of their interests. In the case of CIADEA-Renault, solidarity did not develop along similar lines, but with conditions specific to the case. At first, workers tried to avoid the traditional and ineffective union, voting for the opposition group. They participated as an act of solidarity with other colleagues and as a form of protection of their own threatened rights, in the factory occupation called by the union. But later on, those solidarity links and expectations for a new leader and a new union direction were frustrated by the co-opting of the former opposition and the dilution of conflict negotiated by the company and the union bureaucracy. Given the context of unemployment, this produced fear and divisions and broke the possibility of building action around solidarity.

Third, the two cases analysed also seem to agree, in that mobilization has to be seen as the result of the combination of specific internal conditions. This is true with reference to the causes of the conflict that we have just mentioned. In both cases mobilization appeared as something specific to the factory and to its working situation and labour relations. But the stress on internal conditions does not mean that the external situation did not play any role – it is what produced the foundation on which the internal conditions could be created. The FIAT/SMATA agreement received the support of the national political powers as it represented the first step in introducing labour flexibility in the industrial sector. FIAT received consistent support also from the local political power that expected 20,000 new jobs (both direct and indirect) from the establishment of the new plant in the industrial area of Córdoba. Moreover, the mobilization led by the bureaucratic union at CIADEA-Renault was a reaction imposed by a generalized social protest present in the country at that moment and by the anti-bureaucratic FIAT mobilization. As will be more evident in the next chapter, external conditions would play a fundamental role first in the establishment, consolidation and radicalization of the FIAT workers' mobilization and later on in the company's counter-mobilization and workers' divisions.

We do not want to generalize from these findings, at least we do not want to do it by identifying a 'best model' for workers' collective actions. The combination of factors and conditions influencing the possibility for workers to contest their surrounding social reality are almost endless. Describing new cases and discovering new dynamics are always useful in creating new empirical knowledge and in contributing to existing debates. The cases in this research might have added to this by criticizing the use of the idea of injustice and by presenting a case where the sequential injustice-leadership-collective action is contested.

However important all this may be, it will always remain within contingent explanations. In order to overcome this, this work has been inspired by a different perspective. We wanted to show how structural conditions related to the nature of the capitalist labour process were by themselves *necessary* to workers' collective action. This, far from being a theoretically and intellectually restrictive aim, rediscussing and reconfirming Marxist assumptions on the capitalist labour process, was a necessary departure point to account for – within the system's imposed tendencies and counter-tendencies – for the role and importance of agency factors.

With this objective in mind, by looking at the case of FIAT, the next chapter will take into account on the one hand the role of leadership and organization in strengthening solidarity and accompanying worker radicalization, and on the other, the company's repressive practices in dividing workers and breaking solidarity.

5
Conflict Evolution at FIAT: Workers' Radicalization and Company Repression

Introduction

This chapter follows the evolution and radicalization of conflict at FIAT in the year following the first factory occupation, with three aims in mind: first, to show how leaders emerged from within the context of mobilization and the role they had in catalysing workers' grievances; second, to consider how workers changed themselves while collectively contesting the social reality surrounding them and third, to show how effective the company's counter-mobilization strategies of eliminating leaders, dividing workers and breaking solidarity were.

Following these aims, the chapter is organized into three sections, each analysing in detail the role of the above factors in the outcome of mobilization. A fourth concluding section will locate the same factors in a broad temporal cycle of struggles and counter-struggles by differentiating between the workers' and the company's perspectives. On the one hand by looking at FIAT's workers mobilization as a cycle help to establish links between the role of different agency factors in alternatively hampering and favouring mobilization and thus contributing to a dynamic view of collective action. On the other hand, by outlining the radically different perspectives that guide workers' and company's actions in a cycle of struggle help reconnecting the role of agency factors within the immanency of structural conditions.

In the previous chapter we emphasized that cases of spontaneous action show how objective conditions related to the nature of the capitalist labour process are in themselves not just *necessary* but also *sufficient* to produce collective action. Although far from being the only way in which collective power is expressed, these cases point the needle of our theoretical compass toward structural explanations. However, not all cases follow this pattern and subjective/agency factors, as in the case of leaders, are important in activating collective action or in strengthening the possibility for it to be sustained over time. Would these two assertions be in conflict? Certainly not if we agree that

> *men make their own history, but they do not make it as they please; they do not make it under self-selected circumstances, but under circumstances existing already, given and transmitted from the past.* (Marx 1852, chapter one).

Thus while the importance of subjective factors has to be reconfirmed, two things should be underlined from a theoretical point of view: that if objective conditions are not made explicit, the emphasis on subjective factors alone may provide in the best of cases contingent explanations and in the worst of cases a sublimation of subjectivity, and that however important the role of subjective factors, it would always be set within a system based on existing objective conditions that create contradictions.

With this background clearly in mind, we could say that while the study of the dynamics of mobilization detailed in the previous chapter has been used to highlight cases in which necessary and sufficient conditions for workers' collective action might originate in structural conditions, the evolution of the conflict at FIAT in the year following the first factory occupation that is presented in this chapter will help us to reconsider the role of leaders in strengthening solidarity and that of company repression in breaking it. Overall, this will emphasize the importance of agency factors in shaping the outcomes of workers' mobilizations.

The emergence of leaders

We have argued that the vacuum of power coincident with the change to the new contract allowed the solidarity built in the cooperative labour process to be expressed and activated, and the workers to question the inevitability of the objective reality. Leaders at FIAT emerged from within this solidarity movement, as a result of the mobilization. Within this context, leaders then strengthened solidarity, acting as a catalyst for workers' grievances, proposing solutions to current problems and providing a first stimulus for organization, all by trying to frame a discourse that the majority of people could recognize. But how did these leaders emerge?

The following is a reconstruction of the events from a management perspective:

> *a debate started, in the whole plant there were discussions. After this a movement started to grow, they started to mobilize. They had no idea of where to go and what to do but nonetheless they started to gather, they were many, and then an internal mobilization of the plant, without leaders, started to emerge. In this situation from the same mobilization natural leaders started to appear, these latter were the people with more character, the biggest, the most wicked, the ones who could raise their voices and say let's go. This type of people were those who led the mobilization. Natural and spontaneous leaders started to emerge.*
> (FIAT, former REPO)[68]

Leaders started to emerge from the same mobilization, from the debate in the plant. People did not go to work with the idea of occupying the plant or to protest; there was a general collective feeling that both the company and the union were responsible for their situation but there was no organization, no leadership able to transform individual grievances into collective action. Not even those who later led the process of mobilization had it clearly in mind what to do. A couple of them did not even sign the new contract and went to the plant the day of the occupation to receive their redundancy payments, while others wanted to resign. Nothing was planned but the same situation of uncertainty, impotence and desperation was affecting the majority of workers. The occupation was in a certain way a reflexive act, not in the sense that it was planned before, but that many had reflected, day and night, in discussions with their families and other colleagues on the consequences of the change to the new contract. *'When we signed the new contract the rebellious attitude was not to work, people were thinking, it was terrible, it was just chatting and chatting to see what could be done'* (FIAT activist).[69]

Was solidarity already working?

The day after [the change to the new contract] the guys went to the plant ... that night nobody slept. They went home, they calculated what they were going to receive, they discovered that they were going to earn half of their previous salary for doing the same job, they got depressed, they cried, they didn't sleep. The day after they reached the plant feeling bad, a collective bad feeling and without anybody suggesting anything to them, they got together. What should we do? (FIAT, member of the independent union commission)[70]

Solidarity emerged in this context and, on the basis of the state of mobilization it produced, leaders could find space.

The people who led the mobilization certainly had personal characteristics or useful experience at the time of the action. They had recognition among a group of a few colleagues on the production line, some political activity or experience in social organizations, but almost none had friends among the other leaders and before the conflict they never had any union activity. But three weeks before the factory occupation, some of those who later were recognized by their colleagues as leaders abandoned their workplaces, convinced a number of workers to do the same and went to the union office in the plant. Despite union opposition, an assembly of them decided to abandon work for the day. The protest was spontaneous and was justified by the government's decision to cut the financial assistance each worker was receiving, which was in proportion to the number of his/her children. This action might have alerted management to the possibility that spontaneous protest could emerge again and that the internal commission was largely ineffective in controlling workers. But the company was probably confident of the fact that no organization was available to channel any such protests, that workers at CORMEC were not used to conflict and that many of those wearing the FIAT *camiseta* (shirt) would rather promote their interests through institutional channels, without open conflict.

The company read the situation correctly at least as far as the issue of organization was concerned. Just three weeks between this spontaneous demonstration and the occupation of the factory. Workers could not organize any solid alliance and, as seen from the above quotation, nobody went to the plant the day after the change to the new contract with the idea of mobilizing people or, furthermore, the thought of occupying the plant.

But despite the absence of any form of organization and mutual agreement, leaders emerged spontaneously from the micro context of their department or production line, where discussions among workers had already started. During the morning shift, when the factory was occupied, four leaders emerged, two of whom had participated in the mobilization that had occurred three weeks earlier. Each of them led his own line or a part of it, often with fierce company opposition, and walked with the group of others to lines where workers were still undecided whether to abandon their work or not. The reconstruction of those moments and the function of the leaders are best described by one of those who led the mobilization:

> *That day we were all discussing this and suddenly there was just silence [...] because the feeling was generalized and I became very nervous. In that moment I was [...] I started to punch a keyboard of the machine, I wasn't feeling pain it was just to release my anger. In that moment the foreman passed and sought me, but people were copying me and everyone started hitting and then in all the production lines. In the sector where the engines were tested, people started to remove the silencers. The more I was hitting the keyboards the more the rest were following me.* (Fiat's independent union delegate)[71]

The foreman invited all the production line workers to his office and there he threatened them with the consequences that this act could have on their jobs: they were now workers of FIAT Auto, they had accepted all the conditions of the new contract and had to obey him.

> *I stood up and I turned the table on him and said to him 'Here we are going to do what the mass decides and if the mass decides not to work we are not going to work, is that clear?' 'You are nothing.' 'Yes we are many, we are workers.' 'You don't talk to me in such a way, I am your boss.' 'Now you are nothing and I am going to stand up, I am going out and those who want to follow come with me.' I stood up and everybody followed me.* (Fiat's independent union delegate)[72]

In this brief reconstruction of the events we can see how one of the leaders transformed solidarity into mobilization. He first gave voice to the workers' collective sentiments, making them real through the use of physical violence on the machine, and people followed suit. He then defended his position, and that of the people who were supporting him, against the action of the foreman. In doing this he further framed the workers' grievances, identifying the 'enemy' and the strength and identity of the group (*somos muchos, somos trabajadores,* we are many, we are workers) and then he completed the process of transformation to solidarity by calling for mobilization, and people followed. The construction and the role of leaders in framing the workers' grievances and transforming solidarity into collective action echoes that described in Fantasia's wildcat strike (Fantasia 1988, Ch. 3). As in this latter case, individual leaders from different departments met in the courtyard of the plant. At this time a situation of confusion, fear and indecision was uppermost among people: *'Que hacemos?'* (What can we do?). Once again it was the leadership who offered a solution in a rather fortuitous way, very similar to what happened at the plant described by Fantasia. One of the four who were at that moment leading the mobilization, violently closed the main gate as a way of sharing his anger; it was like a detonation: glass broke into hundreds of pieces, all the people reached the gate and simultaneously the word went out. The plant was occupied.

Here a new and more challenging situation for the original leaders started. All the workers were now concentrated within a few hundred metres and were waiting for some sort of information, some direction to action, and they needed to understand the situation more clearly. The internal commission was not there, having disappeared; the company, having issued the new contract, was not to be believed any more. People started to talk, each one expressing his own point of view, each one identifying those responsible for the situation, and then more workers from the other shifts entered the plant. In this context the leadership grew and nine people were elected. Since a permanent assembly came to be the dominant part of the process of mobilization, a qualitative step in leadership had to be made. Now the problem was to offer, together with a clear understanding of the situation (the frame), a solution with which to confront the company effectively. In such a context of democratic decisions and opposition to bureaucracy, the leaders had to convince people not just to mobilize, this was already a reality, but also to maintain and organize the collective action that had originally been spontaneous. At the same time the anti-bureaucratic stance promoted by the grassroots bulk of the assembly was so strong that the leaders never acted autonomously (although the company pressed for this: with the plant occupied, one of the conditions for the start of negotiations was for the commission to take decisions independently and later submit them to the assembly for ratification); they were delegates and had the power to negotiate certain issues with the company only on the basis of a clear mandate from the assembly. This process of democratic decision-making remained a dominant organizational character in the later radicalization of the mobilization and at the same time was what strengthened it (this will become more evident in the following section). But it is important to stress at this stage that the democratic process established by its status, at least initially, as a permanent assembly, gave a peculiar character to the function of leadership from the beginning. Leaders coordinated, organized and proposed solutions through constant contact with the grassroots.

> *They thought I was a powerful leader because I could transform that mass of lambs, wearing the shirt, into exemplary fighters. But they did this!!! They did it. The only thing I did was to clarify the situation, nothing more than that.* (FIAT's workers elected representative)[73]

While democracy remained as the pattern of the relationship, people followed en masse.

The last quotation and the reference to the fact that management looked at leadership as the 'heart' of the mobilization seem to be confirmed by the media covering of the events, which we mentioned in the previous chapter, analysing the causes of the conflict. The argument was centred on the political background and private life of the person elected by workers as leader as this information was considered fundamental to finding possible solutions of the conflict.

Management emphasis on the leadership can also be found, in what can be defined as a case of mismanagement, in the words of a former foreman: 'I know that, at that moment, they were upset, people in the personnel office were disappointed by the fact that that person, who could have been on the side of the company, was in reality against it' (former CPI, FIAT).[74]

The fact that during the counter-mobilization phase the company focused on weakening and repressing the leadership and in considering it, as the core of mobilization, is an element that invites further reflections on the function of leadership. We have argued that, at least in this case, solidarity emerged out of the workers' interactions in the particular situation created by the change of contract. In this context, leadership should be seen as the element that, born out of a solidarity movement, transformed the same into a solid mobilization that made the workers' grievances explicit. But we could argue that once collective action solidifies into organizational forms, leadership becomes a constituent element of solidarity rather than just a product of it. In this transformation the function of leadership changes and assumes the role of a cohesive element unifying individual perceptions into collective thinking/actions. In a way, we could say that leaders can represent an ideal continuation of the same mobilization that produced them. In this process, as the next section will show, a certain separation from the rank and file is in part inevitable and in part provoked by counter-mobilization. *'In the second factory occupation, activism took a leading role and this broke democratic relations with the rank and file, it was a mistake. Many times the role of activism is to give voice to the anger that each one has in itself'* (independent union member).[75]

The resilience of activism and worker radicalization

'After the factory occupation I met a different type of people, together we became politicized [...], before we were an "island"' (FIAT worker).[76] The shock produced by the change to the new flexible contract and the company's and union's betrayals brought FIAT workers back, following the imagery of an 'island', to the 'mainland' of labour relations. At that time, Argentina, the country that had represented the ideal model of the implementation of neo-liberal policies, started to decline in terms of industrial production and GDP, while social cohesion was becoming unsustainable in a context of rising unemployment and underemployment. In this process of decline, the automotive industry represented, as it often did, the centre around which industrial development could be fostered, employment increased and the government's power strengthened. The FIAT/SMATA agreement was very important because it was the contract whose implementation would have opened the way to the labour flexibility of the entire industrial sector. In 1995–96, SMATA signed similar agreements with

other big companies in the automotive industry and a cascade effect was to be expected in related sectors.

FIAT workers mobilized through the occupation of the plant when the external social climate was certainly favourable to labour conflict. In another section, reference has already been made to this as far as the national level was concerned. In the city of Córdoba, in particular, street demonstrations against the reform of the education system of the province had already, before FIAT's mobilization, gathered together thousands of people. This situation was fundamental in shaping the outcome of the first conflict and labour-management relations in the plant in the next nine months.

For the local newspaper, the conciliation dictated by the provincial ministry of labour, which suspended the plant's occupation and restored the situation to that prior to the change to the new contract, was clearly a recognition of the repercussions the conflict could have had on the entire labour movement in the city: 'There was a risk that the conflict could extend to other plants and that the central act of the protest could have been carried out in front of CORMEC' (*La Voz del Interior*, 24 September 1996).[77] With the factory still occupied and a general strike against labour flexibility called for 26 September, there was a risk that the conflict at FIAT could have been transformed into the centre and symbol of labour protests in the city of Córdoba. Television and radio channels also gave space in their news programmes to what was happening at FIAT. The company's workers were recovering a major role in the local labour movement after decades of passivity, and the majority of the population was supportive of their struggles.

Despite this role acquired among the public and to a certain extent within the Cordoban working class, we do not have to think that FIAT's workers developed, once in contact with the reality around them, a revolutionary character, as reports of the conflict from radical sectors of the Argentine Left seem to show or to hope. Nevertheless, at the same time, they did not use the power they acquired from the mobilization in that particular social situation exclusively for economic demands. They constantly mixed 'bread and butter' issues with more radical objectives, in terms of both representation in the workplace and of their position in society. In the months following the first occupation of the plant, conflict was mainly generated by the company's refusal formally to recognize the new workers' organization. This created a constant push and pull of management and workers. The newly elected leaders promoted a campaign of solidarity with others plants and neighbourhoods, looking for a way to export the conflict out of the gate of the plant. This strategy necessarily involved discussions of the reasons for such actions, and this implied questioning the socio-political system as a whole.

The evolution of the struggle in the FIAT factory may be seen as the evolution of the workers' socio-political consciousness. Struggle against the company, symbolized by its foreign ownership and the newly introduced working practices and salary conditions, went together with the development of a socio-political consciousness, unexpected in a group of workers who were not very familiar with conflict. In this process, the mobilization removed obstacles that had for years hampered the possibility of conflict. As in the case of solidarity and leadership, which emerged spontaneously once the obstacles to their full development disappeared, the workers' consciousness, too, could be seen as a spontaneous outcome of the situation created through the mobilization. The pressure of market competition outdated and bypassed the paternalistic policies of the company and overcame the bureaucratic union's ability to control the labour force. The factors that had inhibited conflict for decades weakened. These elements were no longer of any use in containing workers' protests; solidarity and later on leadership emerged as the most natural bases around which workers' strength could be built.

Opposition to union bureaucracy and company labour flexibility was led from the beginning by an independent and democratic organization that was a direct consequence of the workers' renewed freedom and autonomy. In this context, radicalization could be seen as a systematic element in the evolution of the workers' struggles, just as solidarity was spontaneous the day of the factory occupation.

> *I will never forget when Gallo said: 'We recovered our own power of decisions, the possibility to take decisions.' We recovered the power of struggle, of debate, before nothing was discussed. And the group was so strong...was great.* (FIAT production line worker)[78]

It is important to stress that once we refer to radicalization as a systematic outcome of a process of mobilization, we are not saying that in all cases conflict radicalizes workers. There are particular situations, like the one at FIAT, in which a combination of factors has been so explosive as to overcome and momentarily break those elements that inhibit workers' protests that in the past had worked very well in controlling collective action. In this context of weakened control and increased exploitation, a vacuum was created that allowed the workers' solidarity to be strengthened and alternative forms of organization to be implemented. In the case of CIADEA-Renault, changes were introduced smoothly, workers were divided, the bureaucratic union maintained control and no space for radicalization was left, despite external conditions that could have favoured it.

In the months after the FIAT occupation, the workers' elected leaders tried to foster, despite company opposition, the structure of their organization and in January 1997, after several unsuccessful attempts to be recognized as an independent local branch of SMATA, they formed an independent union, SITRAMF. This signalled the highest level of their anti-bureaucratic opposition and at the same time the point of no return in their conflict with the company. Independent of the support that the majority of workers gave to the new organization and continuous attempts to establish solidarity links outside the factory, company counter-mobilization weakened the possibility for keeping the workers actively mobilized. As admitted by a former REPO, while apparently emphasizing managerial involvement strategies: *'People started to be really identified with the teamwork and we could recover the plant. Leaders lost support and left the plant... well we fired them'* (FIAT, former REPO).[79]

Divisions emerged regarding the strategies to be used in the conflict, and both the fear of losing a job and company pressure pushed many to retire from active conflict. Moreover, divisions apart, the change in the workers' consciousness had already produced a continuing incompatibility and non-conformity with working in the factory. One year after the first factory occupation, 1200 out of 1700 workers who had signed the new agreement with FIAT were laid off, forced to abandon the plant and replaced. At that time, after a year of struggle and the elimination of leaders and activists, it was *'impossible to regain control of the people. Many of them had to leave, there was no more possibility of their identification with the compromise. They were laid off or they voluntarily left'* (FIAT, former REPO).[80]

There are several factors, both internal and external, that could explain the resilience of the workers' resistance and opposition. The socio-political conditions at the time of the conflict offered a set of examples of other mobilizations and the forms through which a more effective response could be offered. FIAT workers received solidarity from organizations already involved in a process of opposition to labour flexibility and privatization. Political parties and public opinion, as well, offered support for their struggle because this contributed to discrediting the overall political project promoted by Menem. In general, the situation at the time of the conflict represented the context in which workers at FIAT could start their struggle, and provided fertile soil for extending it out of the factory. Solidarity developed with anti-bureaucratic movements in other plants, as was the case of Renault before the internal opposition was co-opted, actions in defence of poor neighbourhoods and the establishment of relations with union organizations in other FIAT factories worldwide. But although this scenario could have influenced a radicalization of conflict positively, the majority of those interviewed agreed with the view that they were basically struggling alone. Many workers and their organizations openly supported the struggle at FIAT, but government and the union bureaucracies boycotted it and the fear of job losses hampered extensive solidarity from other factories. In the country as a whole there were many acts of resistance but they were scattered, with no central representation, and no political party was willing or able to act in defence of the same struggles. 'We were feeling, and it was in reality like this, that we were alone, we were the first' (independent union delegate):[81]

> We told other workers: 'They are going to cut your salary', they replied 'No I don't think so'. You don't get involved until it really happens to you. When we went to the Chevrolet plant, workers went out from the back door and nobody came closer to chat with us. (FIAT worker)[82]

The sense of abandonment that emerges from the interviews and the fact that FIAT's workers were basically alone in their conflict indicate that we should not underestimate the internal conditions that generated the mobilization as a possible basis and explanation of radicalization. Nonetheless, external conditions made for a social scenario in which labour conflict was certainly favoured, and these conditions found a fertile soil in the specific circumstances that led to mobilization.

The same elements that fostered the emergence of solidarity and then leadership also created the conditions in which a more radical opposition could be developed. In this sense the shock provoked by the change of contract and the anger against the company and the unions were both the basis of the first mobilization and of its radicalization and establishment. Workers were now free to express their opinions and to channel their demands through an organization that was really defending them; they could stand up with dignity and refuse the foremen's impositions. They were feeling proud to have defended themselves after years of passivity.

> *The company couldn't control us any more. Everything was a batucada, hitting the machine, we did batucada for every type of reason. The will of the people wasn't the same. The 'elderly' who were used to set the machine didn't want to do it any more for that amount of money. People gradually became rebels.* (FIAT worker)[83]

> *The plant was really out of control, it was as I am telling you, workers could do what they wanted, they worked as they liked and these people* (the leaders) *really had the pulse of people, because people were really angry. They didn't want these nine leaders but rather they were disappointed and angry and were showing it through this action.* (FIAT, former REPO)[84]

Internal and external conditions, with reference to their effects on radicalization, are probably not mutually exclusive and for what has been argued until now could be seen as complementary. In an attempt to put together the pieces that make up a process of mobilization, it may be useful to think of solidarity and consciousness as two succeeding points in a continuous line of evolution/radicalization in which leadership and organization have filtered, framed and established a connection between the internal and external worlds. If the process of mobilization is positioned in this temporarily broadened perspective, the role and importance of leadership and organization in the same process appear much clearer than through a narrow focus on a single mobilization event. At the same time, as the case of CIADEA-Renault shows, less successful cases of mobilization/radicalization can be explained as well. In that company, in the particular situation previously described, leadership and organization did not play any important role in framing the workers' consciousness; rather, they contained it. In other words radicalization, as far as the case of FIAT is concerned, seems to constitute that level of the process of mobilization in which solidarity has been already transformed, through action, into consciousness. The following quotations evidence how this process of transformation occurred contemporarily with the evolution of the struggle:

> *When we occupied the plant for the first time we really didn't have a clear consciousness of what we were doing.* (FIAT production line worker)[85]

> *People were now different, the same person was not the same as before, he could see the world in a different way, he had 'jumped' and this happened to all of us, to all of us. The same struggle changed us, all of us, it changed us, it shaped us, it changed me and all of us. Emotion, I could say, in our case, was an essential element in our struggle.* (FIAT workers' elected representative)[86]

> *We were part of it, we were in the middle of it. In that moment we started to realize what labour flexibility was and what was going to happen in the country.* (FIAT worker)[87]

> *During this process that lasted one, one and half years, a very big change in consciousness occurred, and this despite the different position each one took at the moment of struggle.* (FIAT worker, production line)[88]

The above quotations seem to confirm that radicalization and a change of consciousness were part of an evolution in the process of mobilization. At the same time, this evolution was not perceived by the actors as a clear and unequivocal perspective. People radicalized in and through the struggle, became activists because, day by day, they had to defend themselves and what they had achieved. The rhythm and the time of the conflict set the quality and the level of the workers' consciousness. Company repression forced some of the workers to retire from activism, and contributed to increasing a sense of group identification in both those who continued the open confrontation and those who did not. The conditions in which mobilization emerged favoured radicalization as an evolution in the workers' collective consciousness detached from clear cost and benefit calculations.

In this sense, the case of FIAT and its outcomes is far from any rational choice theory or approach. Is there anything rational in the decision to occupy the plant and provoke the company so openly when less costly actions could have been implemented instead (for instance a strike or a union negotiation)? Is there any self-interested individual decision that could be detected in the dynamic of the workers' mobilization? Did they individually reflect on the costs and benefits of their action before it was put into practice? People who in the last two decades had been used to thinking for themselves were identified with the company and had no confidence in collective action. Did they then act, in the case of this mobilization, irrationally?

As previously shown, internal and external conditions influenced the process of mobilization differently. A particular combination of factors created a fertile soil for the workers' collective action and this was not the product of picket lines, the union's coercion or any other form of instrumentalization of the workers' individual wills. The evidence in our case pointed to the fact that collective action emerged spontaneously. Solidarity appeared as the natural basis around which a group of people, angered and betrayed by the union and the company, found its strength; the leadership filtered and framed the grievances; activism kept people mobilized and the conflict radicalized. People's solidarity changed into socio-political consciousness evolving through, and in, action.

The change in consciousness is fundamental to understanding why, despite the adverse conditions of the struggle, FIAT workers continued in their action although they were aware that there was a high probability of losing the conflict and their jobs.

After the first factory occupation, the group of leaders who were elected during the mobilization kept representing the workers with the company, despite management never officially recognizing the new organization.

> *The company never recognized them* (the elected leaders) *from a legal point of view, we always treated them as a fact, as a factual representation. In other words, if they were those with whom we had to discuss that's fine, we talked. But we never recognized them as trade union. They always demanded such recognition but the company always denied it. For us the trade union was SMATA.* (FIAT, former REPO)[89]

In the three months that followed the first conflict a semi-clandestine union was formed and its relations with the company were of daily confrontation. Apart from the struggle for formal recognition, with SMATA boycotting it, the new flexible labour conditions were the main reasons for the constant state of conflict. This situation favoured more political debate among workers through small assemblies, and small discussions organized by the group of nine who led the first mobilization and another 70 delegates. During these meetings the possibility of defeat was taken into consideration:

> *we never said we were going to lose, of course nobody struggles if he doesn't see a possibility of winning, but we debated, and we voted in an assembly that losing was a possibility and that if we would had lost the conflict they were going to fire all of us. And we had to opt and this was very important. We gave people the possibility of resigning. We looked around and we considered that resignation was one possibility and that the other was to struggle. If we wanted to struggle we had to do it well, if we wanted to resign as well. Nothing in the middle. In that situation resign meant bend your head [...] not just to accept Menem. Menem came together with other losses. The company was gradually trying to introduce new conditions, after the occupation it wanted to recover the space it had lost. We had to consider that fact.* (FIAT workers' elected representative)[90]

A similar discussion preceded the second factory occupation, which was justified as a reaction to the laying off of one of the elected union commission members. Many opposed it, but the majority voted in favour because it was the only way to show the company the strength of the union and to defend its future existence. In the second factory occupation, too, the risk was calculated but the decision was certainly not based on individual gain. At least for those who actively participated, the issues were the defence of a collective interest and the future existence of the union. The company was clearly trying to weaken the new union and workers were individually under pressure from foremen not to participate. Job advancements were proposed to those who were not involved in any action, and the possibility of being fired was constant.

> *...foremen used to call me activist. Why are you calling me activist? Because I'm saying the truth? Because I'm fighting to protect what is*

*my right? They tried to smash you so to push you to resign to your job.
They called me in their offices many times but I didn't want to leave so
they fired me.* (FIAT production worker)[91]

*Foremen used to tell you that they had seen you talking with the guys of
the union and that this was going to create problems for you, that it was
better not to do it anymore.* (FIAT production worker)[92]

Despite this company strategy of dividing workers who were in
action, half of them occupied the plant and defied it, provoking further retaliation. The sacked union commission member could not be
reinstated and the conflict ended with 42 new layoffs.

Repression and counter-mobilization

The role of repression as the main instrument available to companies in counter-mobilization is very well documented and represented
by the case of FIAT. Cases of physical aggression were not recorded,
but the use of psychological methods occurred daily. According to
those interviewed, the mobilization's leaders and their families were
shadowed by company security agents, activists were moved to the
night shifts and promotion was given to those who wanted to abandon the 'rebels'. The company could also influence the media, just
by threatening television and newspapers with the suspension of
adverts. During the first occupation of the plant, which occurred
over the spring equinox, a local radio station suggested that the
workers' wives, who were with their husbands in the plant day and
night, find a different way to celebrate the new season. But the evidence of the use of repressive methods is just one aspect of a more
general approach used by companies to deal with workplace conflict. As stated by FIAT's industrial relations director in a co-authored
academic journal article, in the Argentine case the strategy adopted
was similar to that used in Italy during the 1970s (in the so called
conflittività permanente, continuous conflict): 'The dismissals of the
most violent activists have had a symbolic character and have re-
established internal order and management prerogatives' (Camuffo
and Massone 2001, p. 68).[93]

The respect for internal order and management prerogatives in the
control of the labour process has been, and is, the principle and the
leitmotif always stressed by companies all over the world. Workplace

case studies have frequently shown, even if not always directly, the centrality of the control of labour and the use of coercion, in the study and understanding of the dynamics of industrial relations and collective action (see for instance Beynon 1984; Fantasia 1988; Milkman 1997). It is true that there is a certain level of worker consent in the exploitation of labour, as Burawoy discovered, but this co-exists with coercion. At the same time, it is important to stress that companies are not alone in the use of repression to control workers' protests and that states are often willing participants. The historical perspective presented in the previous chapter could show how, for instance in the case of Argentina, state repression has been widely used.

In addition, in looking at repression and considering its role in the mobilization process, it is necessary to specify the different meanings that the same concept can have. The cases analysed seem to suggest that repression can assume a more direct, explicit and violent form or it can be used in a less evident way, through more camouflaged action, without explicit acts of violence. This distinction corresponds to the use of repression directly against mobilization events or as an instrument for the prevention of conflict. The difference is particularly important in understanding how it influenced solidarity and the evolution of the workers' consciousness.

FIAT, like CIADEA-Renault, used all the methods available to break the workers' solidarity, to divide them, to make them loyal and obedient once again (*la familia FIAT*). Direct repression, as far as the case of FIAT is concerned, was fundamental as an obstacle to further mobilization. But at the same time, it produced radicalization of the conflict and encouraged the faster development of the workers' consciousness. In the case of CIADEA-Renault, repression did not operate explicitly because SMATA's co-opting of rank and file opposition provided the company with the best instrument for controlling the labour force and for continuing the implementation of labour flexibility and outsourcing. CIADEA-Renault, probably in the light of FIAT's experience, avoided direct confrontation, and implemented changes slowly, with union complicity.

In the case of FIAT, many elements (how the abrupt changes of salary and working conditions impacted on the workers' sense of loyalty to the enterprise, union betrayal and the negation of the social development that many identified with working for the company) contributed to reinforcing solidarity directly through action without an established organization and leadership. These two components stabilized in the first three months after the first mobilization when the workers' solidarity transformed itself, under the act of organization and leadership, into a new and a deeper socio-political consciousness. Moreover, for this reason company repression had to be far more radical than the simple elimination of the leaders. One year after the first plant occupation, 1200 out of the 1700 workers who had signed the new contract with FIAT had been made redundant. A change in consciousness had already happened. In the case of CIADEA-Renault, where an active and challenging rank and file movement came under the control of the traditional union, workers did not progress in their socio-political consciousness. They felt impotent regarding the company, the union and the political power. In the years after their mobilization they lived in fear of losing their jobs and with a pervasive sense of impotence and frustration, knowing that almost every day colleagues at work were fired (suspended) and that it would probably be their turn next. Similarly some of the FIAT workers who remained in the plant after the 'cleansing' later blamed themselves for not having participated in the mobilizations much more then they did; after this process of consciousness-raising, their lives in the plant and their relations with the company changed completely.

These two different forms of repression, a 'direct' counter-mobilization and 'indirect' preventive one, could work effectively within a legal context that was not protective of workers' independent union activity. We have already referred to the system for union recognition, its dependency on political decisions and how powerful the influence of traditional bureaucratic unions in such matters can be. The intervention of the provincial government as mediator between the two sides is also questionable. In the case of FIAT, especially, a company that had plans to hire 5000 new workers, power relations have to be taken into consideration even if we believe that all the rules have been respected and no doubts are raised about the honesty of government executives. In the case of the second factory occupation, the intervention of the provincial ministry of labour, annulling the effects of all the actions taken during the conflict, should have reversed the 41 layoffs used by the company to repress activism. Through an interpretation open to debate, the conflict was not considered as collective and the firings were regarded as individual sanctions to be resolved in front of a tribunal. This action in practice supported company repression.

Last, but not least, the case of FIAT, as already mentioned, coincided with the introduction of flexible contracts in the industrial sector. The implementation of the contract was considered as a kind of test both for the other multinationals of the sector and for the government of Menem, who emphasized labour flexibility as a panacea for unemployment and for his own credibility. Menem was expected in Córdoba for the opening of the new plant, but according to the local newspaper his decision not to participate was dependent not on his health conditions but rather on fear of public protests in the province and in the FIAT plant (*La Voz del Interior*, 19 December 1996). Workers were not willing to welcome the person they saw as responsible for their situation and threatened the management that they would mobilize on the day of the opening if the president came. According to several interviews, during the days of the first occupation voices were saying in the plant that police repression was imminent.

The data also show samples of different forms of repression. The firing of activists was the most obvious method used by the company and aimed to weaken the workers' resistance through the elimination of their leaders. A more subtle way was to overburden or move to the worst section of the production line those workers who had participated in mobilization. This served to create conditions of severe stress and isolation, which acted psychologically on the capacity for resistance of these workers. People were forced in this way to give up their jobs and the company could use this 'voluntary decision' as proof that no firings were under way and that in reality workers were freely abandoning their jobs. Foremen and REPO introduced a climate of fear, suspicion and threats in the factory for all those who maintained friendship and support with the people outside the plant.[94] Being a former CORMEC worker meant being considered a rebel, and workers at the new plant were kept at a distance from the possibility of 'perversion'. At the same time the action of the company was inflexible in its recognition of SMATA as the only legitimate representation of its employees and the use of this form of legalized repression gave no chance to the recently formed independent union.

Repression can assume different meanings and forms, and be promoted by the company, the state and the legal system, alone or in combination and through more or less direct intervention. In all these cases its fundamental roles are to break solidarity, to divide workers through an individualization of the employment relationship and of certain benefits and to prevent collective action. Repression is a natural instrument available to companies not just to counter-mobilize and eliminate activists and leaders, but also to impose managerial decisions, the respect for internal order and managerial prerogatives, to use the words of FIAT's industrial relations director. This kind of repression is the most subtle and difficult to grasp, because the logic of the management's 'right to manage' is the centre of the social system in which we live. To challenge this 'right' means to question the entire system. The decisions of the company, and its right to impose them, will be always justified by the logic of the market, by international competition and by trade agreements. Since no alternative is offered, the impersonal action of the market – the need to be competitive – will always provide a valid reason to legitimize management's 'right' to manage.

The cases of FIAT and CIADEA-Renault have to be seen in this light. Both companies implemented labour flexibility and technological changes because international competition was pressing them to reduce the cost of labour. Workers had somehow to be convinced to accept a reduction in their salaries or precariousness in their employment. It was natural that people used to having a certain standard of living opposed any decision that could have affected this. In both cases, workers mobilized for the same reasons, but specific conditions in the two plants (company strategies and the actions of union bureaucracies) produced different types of mobilization and, consequently, different types of repression: direct as a counter-mobilization in the case of FIAT and indirect, more subtle, but nonetheless effective, in the case of CIADEA-Renault.

Conclusions: a cycle of conflict through workers' and company perspectives

The purpose of this concluding section is to look at FIAT's workers' mobilization as a whole, cyclical process, in which different stages and relations between factors can be identified. This process, however, will appear different depending on the agent's point of view with two radically opposed perspectives emerging. Thus in this section, through the help of a graphic and based on the case analysed, I will attempt to look at both the workers' and the company's perspectives on the conflict (see Figures 5.1 and 5.2). This is particularly important, as the evolution of conflict at FIAT paradigmatically shows not just the tendency and counter-tendency that capital imposes on workers' collective action, but also the possibility for workers' emancipation through practice.

The cycle of conflict from the workers' perspective Here we start with an apparently committed workforce whose aspirations seem to increase due to the expectations the new company's plant is creating; reality contrasts with this, workers do not want a reduction in their living standards; within the collapse of the system that is keeping workers out of conflict solidarity emerges from within the workplace, the factory is occupied; building on solidarity and through practice, democratic leadership creates and formalizes the workers' representative organization; workers are divided, open conflict ends but the practice of struggle has changed workers, the majority have to leave their jobs; the cycle ends, workers are once again, apparently, committed.

Cycle of conflict through company's perspective Here the first stage is represented by an obedient workforce, a necessary condition for company's profitability; under the pressure of increasing global competition and with the need to adopt new technological platforms, the company changes work and salary conditions abruptly;

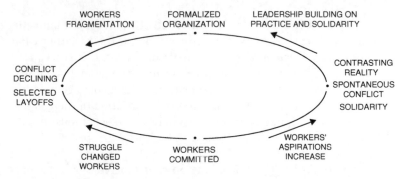

Figure 5.1 The cycle of conflict from the workers' perspective

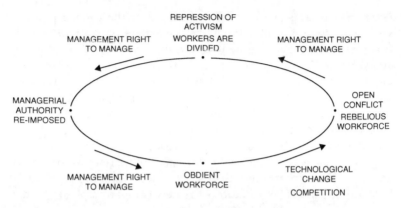

Figure 5.2   The cycle of conflict from the company's perspective

conflict explodes, the company is uncertain on how to deal with a now rebellious workforce; management right's to manage is reaffirmed, divisions among workers are created; repression starts by targeting leaders and activists; managerial authority is reimposed, and the remaining workers return to obedience.

Looking at workers' mobilization from this double perspective is important both analytically and theoretically. Analytically it is useful to account for the complexity of collective action by explaining differences in terms of outcomes as the expression of a combination of diverging forces driving the actions of workers and companies. Theoretically it forces us to focus on the deep content of these driving forces. In this latter perspective,

> a necessary condition for the existence of capital is its ability to divide and separate workers in order to defeat them. Rather than a contingent, incidental characteristic of capital, this is an inner tendency of capital. In capitalism as a whole, the two sided totality, capital does not merely seek the realization of its own goal, valorization; it also must seek to suspend the realization of the goals of wage-labour. Capital, in short, must defeat workers; it must negate its negation in order to posit itself. (Lebowitz 2003, p. 122)

The case of FIAT is just one of the possible outcomes and it seems important to reconfirm here that we do not want to generalize from this. But, with the absence of a trade union as mediating agent and its substitution with forms of direct worker participation, the different interests driving the actions of the company and the workers have always manifested in a direct and open confrontation, thus showing empirically how the diverging forces driving capital and labour have first created and later destroyed workers' mobilization.

6
Conclusions

Collective action as a process

We can see a logic in the responses of similar occupational groups undergoing similar experiences, but we cannot predicate any law. Consciousness of class arises in the same way in different times and places, but never in exactly the same way (Thompson 1980, p. 9). Thompson's methodological and epistemological observation about the historical unfolding of class and class-consciousness, with his emphasis on processes and dynamics, has informed the way in which collective action has been framed both theoretically and empirically in this book.

Collective action is shaped differently by different factors, conditions and contexts, resulting in a potentially infinite number of cases. Favourable socio-political conditions, internal organizational strength, management despotism, workers' explicit confrontational strategies, charismatic leaderships and political parties' guidance and workers' consciousness, bargaining power and technological and skills levels are just a few examples of factors that alone or in combination influence workers' decisions to act collectively. But contrary to the possibility of deriving from this the idea of an inevitably contingent nature of collective action, this book has instead attempted to focus on how the contradictory dynamics of the capitalist labour process creates the necessary conditions for workers' collective action.

Theoretically, rather than focusing on the category of injustice and on the leader-led sequence of injustice-collective action, solidarity has instead been considered as crucial in a reformulation of a theory of collective action. Solidarity exists in the daily interaction of working people, generated by the necessarily cooperative nature of the capitalist labour process, but this existence of solidarity should always be seen as a process, as something in the making, susceptible to external circumstances and forces produced by the contradictory nature of work relations within capitalism.

Empirically, through the comparative analysis of two cases of mobilization, the evidence has pointed to the inadequacy of injustice as the *conditio sine qua non* of workers' collective action and has shown the process through which solidarity is transformed by workers' spontaneous action into its active form, becoming the basis of further mobilization and the radicalization of struggle at FIAT and, in parallel, the target of the company's repression.

Within this dynamic framework, a number of factors, specific to the cases, may be identified as having had a profound influence in terms of collective action outcomes. At FIAT, the abrupt change of contract left workers first astonished, then perplexed and finally angry. They felt betrayed by the trade union's internal commission, which had promised to keep the salary reduction within 10 per cent; they felt abandoned by the company whose paternalistic policies could not resist the pressure of international competition. They spontaneously occupied the plant and soon established their own representation and organization within the vacuum of power created by the contemporary absence of both the union and the company. In the case of Renault, conflict was diluted through clear managerial strategies of gradual workforce reduction and outsourcing of production sections. The bureaucratic union SMATA covertly supported the decisions of the company and kept its leadership unaltered, first controlling and then co-opting internal opposition. The mobilization at FIAT, whose workforce was legally with SMATA, and the Renault workers' protests put pressures on the union leadership and a factory occupation took place.

Of course it is fundamental to know what actually provoked a particular mobilization, the subjects involved and the external and internal influences on the process. The use of comparisons can help to establish a set of rules, or tendencies toward mobilization. This latter point, in particular, has to be treated cautiously. Historical evidence, at least for what concerns Argentina, shows that mobilization does not always respond to predetermined criteria. With a focus on process, fluidity in our interpretation must be maintained.

With this clearly in mind, we can argue that the comparison provides evidence of a dynamic, specific to the cases, in which company strategies and union bureaucracy are the factors that can explain mobilization. But, however important these factors may be in hampering or influencing workers' decisions to act, we cannot easily generalize from these and establish secure patterns for the origin and development of mobilization, but rather we can point at tendencies.

In the case of FIAT, the particular way in which the company and the trade union's internal commission managed the change of contract, at first provided fertile soil for the workers' spontaneous occupation and successively, in what can be defined as a cycle of resistance and counter-resistance, a parallel process of the radicalization of the workers' consciousness and repressive company action.

This parallel process can be an indication of a tendency common to other cases of worker mobilization. Green (1990), for instance, from the perspective of criminal sociology, shows the potential amplifier effects of policing on miners' consciousness, using the case of the 1984–85 strike in Britain. Although in the case of FIAT no direct police repression was used, psychological violence by means of threats and discrimination for all those involved in the conflict was normal and put consistent pressure on workers. Green's analysis goes very close to what I have argued on the issue of repression and consciousness in Chapter 5, arguing that mobilization is a process based on solidarity that transforms the people involved, changing their passivity and individualism into collective action.

The case of FIAT shows a direct link in workers' reactions to the repressive measures adopted by the company. On the one hand, the elimination of leaders and activists weakened the organizational structure, rendering any form of possible resistance increasingly difficult. On the other, those who did not refuse to abandon the conflict strengthened their solidarity links and accepted the risk of a protracted confrontation. The internal struggles with the company and the rhythms and the times of the conflict set the quality and the level of workers' consciousness.

This consciousness changed in and throughout the entire mobilization, affecting the majority of workers who, even if they gradually abandoned open confrontation and activism, had already 'jumped' into a different vision of their reality with regard to both the work-place and the society as a whole. One year after the occupation of the factory 1200 out of 1700 of them had lost their jobs because, as a manager said, they could not accept the 'compromise' any more.

A radical approach to workers' collective action

The perspective adopted in this book has privileged a radical approach and method of research. Radical means here both to go to the roots of the problem and to express a view of workers' organizing that goes beyond trade unions as institutions.

As to the first aspect, I think it is nowadays increasingly more important to reuse Marx's insights into the nature of the labour process and the functioning of capitalism in general to understand issues of workers' collective action. I am not here suggesting following any apologetic version or exegetic analysis of Marx's work. Marxists have probably criticized Marx more than non-Marxists: weaknesses in his thought exist and should not been dismissed (Hyman 2006). The free wage labourer who has nothing other to sell than his/her labour power, identified by Marx as the prototype of worker:

> for a long while, it probably seemed self-evident; it seemed to cor-respond to the process by which a proletariat was formed in the North Atlantic Region. Yet Marx's hypothesis in truth presumes two highly questionable ideas, namely that labour power should be offered for sale by the worker who is the *carrier* and *possessor* of this labour power, and that the workers who sells his or her own labour power *sells nothing else*. (Van der Linden 2008, p. 19, emphasis in original)

While in its historical development capitalism has made, and is currently making, use of a combination of different kinds of worker and labour relations (including indentured labour and slavery), depending on the geographical and historical conditions it encoun-tered in its expansion, revolutions in technology are constantly and in a contradictory manner destroying and creating new skills, new labour relations and new identities, and displacing, dividing and then re-aggregating workers. The space in which Marx's insights into the nature of the labour process can be used is thus profoundly dif-ferent from the one he was describing 150 years ago. However, in so far as the labour process remains an activity done collectively by a group of workers who have been forced to sell their labour and whose activity is externally directed and controlled, there will always be, in here, the basis for their future resistance.

> As soon as subaltern workers are subordinated to a heteronomous labour relationship – which they are by definition – an uninterrupted battle with the employers and their representatives is the result, carried on sometimes openly and sometimes secretly, sometimes individually and sometimes collectively. (Van der Linden 2008, p. 173)

These various forms of resistance reflect both the degree of workers' autonomy from capital domination and the level of their dependency on capitalist forms of work to survive, generating, accordingly, different scales of accommodation and participation. Taking this variability into consideration is very important as it adds complexity to our understanding of collective action. However, against the risk of a sublimation of contingency, it is always fundamental to locate the origin of collective action in the contradictory logic generated within the capitalist labour process, namely, that while requiring a minimum level of cooperation for capital profitability, it also provides the material conditions that favour the collective association of workers and the establishment of solidarity links among them.

There is a second dimension in which I think going to the roots of the problem, as Marx did with his analysis of capitalism, is fundamental. Workers' collective action is as much the result of existing structural conditions on which such action is set, as it is the result – the by-product – of the attempts to reveal and communicate the inner nature of capital mystification. This is a further reason for my critique of injustice, when I argue that it is set within capital's fetishism. The use of this subjective and morally grounded concept, although to a certain extent useful in an organizing perspective/ strategy, is not appropriate in the formulation of a general theory of collective action. By taking for granted that capitalism produces collective action and thus that the necessary conditions for the latter are always in place, this approach entails the implicit disappearance of structural conditions from the analysis and an explicit overreliance on individually based explanations. In contrast, and as developed in this book, solidarity, intended as the social relation that expresses the collective nature of the labour process, is a concept better equipped to explain collective action. Solidarity is indeed at the intersection between, mutually influencing, social structure and social agency and thus epitomizes Marx's idea of conscious human activity as the mediating factor in the unity between the objective and the subjective spheres.

> Solidarity is created and expressed by the process of mutual association. Whether or not a future society is consciously envisioned, whether or not a 'correct' image of the class structure is maintained, the building of solidarity in the form, and in the process of, mutual association can represent a practical attempt to restructure, or reorder, human relations. (Fantasia 1988, p. 11)

The rediscovery of solidarity is crucial not just to identifying the labour process-rooted origins of worker mobilization, but also to think about a radical view of workers' organizing that goes beyond trade unions as institutions.

This is not something new if one thinks of Rosa Luxemburg's argument about the self-activity of workers in the mass strike or of Gramsci's call for workers to participate in work councils and in the takeover of production. It is not new, but it is very often forgotten that, prior to the establishment of stable workers' organizations and very often in parallel with the existence of these, workers do organize and act spontaneously, by developing forms of mutual association, as the simplest and most direct way of defending their interests in the workplace. Through the cases of research and historical analysis of labour conflict in Argentina, in particular, the book has emphasized the importance of starting from workers' self-activity for both collective action and workers' organizing theory. Workers' self-activity is certainly just one of the ways in which they have resisted under capitalism; it is often limited in time, unorganized and not always effective. The importance of recognized leaders and formal structures in workers' organizations in framing action and resistance is doubtless another important historical tendency. But the search for workers' emancipation necessarily passes through forms and processes that may encapsulate workers' self-activity.

Thus, while in this book models of collective action are explicitly criticized, as with what I have called the model of institutionalized collective action centred on trade unions and strikes, grassroots forms of resistance based on solidarity represent an historical general tendency in workers' collective action and express the power of their self-organization.

There is undoubtedly a big distance between ideas and reality. How could we imagine a workers' organizing strategy based on communicating and revealing to workers the power of self-organization and solidarity, since the latter is for many workers an empty word or, even worse, the rhetorical construction of some union leaders and politicians? The reality for many workers is that they are divided while working together, in competition in the labour market and opposed as groups in society and depending overall on capital to live. However, the history of the labour movement is also the history of unceasing workers' collective struggles. These create a fertile soil for people to understand the existing clash of interest between capital and labour but, 'given that the spontaneous response of people in motion does not in itself go beyond capital, communication of the essential nature of capitalism is critical to its non reproduction' (Lebowitz 2004).

In this sense, the theory of collective action presented in this book, emphasizing the importance of solidarity and self-organizing, is more an attempt to use the communication of knowledge as a way to empower workers than a predefined model or strategy for trade union' organizing.

Lessons from Argentina?

The historical analysis of workers' and social mobilizations in Argentina is very rich in cases and experiences that leave no room for doubts as to the importance the country has for all those who study events of collective action and popular uprisings. Whatever the government, the party in power, the ideological framework, the temporal dimension, the level of organization or the charisma of leaders, Argentineans have always, and stubbornly, I am tempted to say, mobilized. This heterogeneity of examples puts under severe scrutiny the validity of any static formulation of mobilization theory in both micro and macro perspectives. Certain conceptual categories and their interrelations may be questioned, assumptions tested and the evidence of new cases considered.

As far as this research is concerned, there are elements that it may be useful to evaluate in a different light: the role of traditional unions as organizers of protest and the relations between external and internal conditions for workers' mobilizations. Especially when we compare the Argentinean case with that of western Europe, the image of trade unions as responsible and 'rational' institutions that are part of a system of industrial relations becomes less clear and precise. Peronism empowered these organizations, transforming them into political and electoral machines, but at the same time workers always maintained strong pressure on leaders for the fulfilment of their needs and demands. This double function as mass organizers for both political and class interests coincided with their power as mobilizers. But the contradictions between Peronist ideology and workers' needs often produced grassroots movements that confronted the power of bureaucracy, once again, in their capacity to mobilize the workforce. This dynamic has strongly influenced labour relations in Argentina, at least from the second part of the twentieth century on, and has shaped people's cultural references and understanding of politics: it is not untrue to say that mobilization is quite a familiar concept for the majority of Argentineans.

The existence of this sort of structural idea of mobilization goes with the economic instability that has characterized Argentina in the historical period under consideration, and particularly in the last decades. As for many peripheral countries, during the 1990s, a programme of privatization, labour flexibility and neoliberal restructuring were implemented under the auspices of the IMF. The results of these 'therapies' were visible worldwide during the popular uprising of December 2001, but this was just the tip of the iceberg. Mobilization started well in advance middle class 'cazerolas revolution' occupied the street of Buenos Aires claiming back their savings. Analysing the situation at FIAT and Renault in 1996, with the knowledge of the events that have happened since, gives us a perspective on a medium period of time during which the socio-political conditions for mobilization emerged gradually and at different times. 'We were the first' said one of FIAT's workers' elected representatives, showing a newspaper reporting *piqueteros* roadblocks in the outskirts of Córdoba. The flexibility of working conditions in the industrial sector was the second target of the reforms introduced under Menem's governments – the first attack had been on workers' rights, put in place during the waves of privatization of former state enterprises. But it is true that the formal sector in Argentina started to decline at approximately the same time, and this created a mass of unemployed people whose only resources for survival, to guarantee their material survival, was mobilization. Those who went on strike at FIAT and Renault, and in similar industrial areas of the country, almost contemporaneously were not starving but were defending an achieved level of social needs, and framed their mobilization within this concrete threat to their rights. Although situated in a period of generalized social unrest, workers' struggles at FIAT and Renault remained largely isolated from the rest of the protests. All of these considerations seem to suggest that waves of mobilization may coincide and be favoured by moments of economic recession but, at least in the cases presented, internal workplace dynamics determines the conditions for mobilization. Thus, while evaluating the perspectives for widespread mobilization, even just by referring to the national context, the tendency for struggles to be fragmented has to be considered. Worker solidarity may be a powerful resource for mobilization, as I have tried to show, but it has to be considered with reference to the situation of a particular group of workers. People at FIAT realized they 'were the first' only when they mobilized, when they became conscious and it was not a surprise for them to be almost alone in their struggle. Despite political calls for solidarity, the cases show that in situations of economic recession what counts is often a short-term perspective based on the satisfaction of immediate needs.

The struggles of the 1990s, although scattered, with a short-term vision and limited in nature, remained as part of the social experience of those who mobilized, and for those unaffected at the time were the signals of an unstable economic system, and the examples and the breeding ground for those who were organizing the new forms of resistance, which have appeared in the last few years. In Argentina, new proletarians have emerged from the ashes of formal employment; traditional industrial conflict has to a certain extent changed its forms but overall the strength of working people's mobilizations has not decreased.

Final considerations

The research presented in this book remains far from an objective, true and 'certified' reality and requires, in the future, the addition of more cases and evidence for the study of mobilization. FIAT and Renault still remain two of the potentially infinite number of cases that could reach the same, or totally different, conclusions. In this book I have simply offered an interpretation of reality on the base of the data in my possession, trying to link empirical factors with deeper theoretical insights.

As I said, many factors in different combinations and dynamics can potentially influence workers' collective action. New research that can add to this by discovering, for instance, the importance of gender (the absence of women representing a structural limitation of this research) for recruitment and mobilization would be more than welcome. However, in the social sciences and in case study research in particular, there is a sort of passion for details and micro conditions, an extreme attention to the correct balance of all the possible factors involved, an abuse of categories and definitions that can sometimes produce the perception that what we are describing is, to be frank, almost an abstraction from reality. This tendency of extreme empiricism and to debate just on 'facts' inevitably leaves out those elements that could also contribute to understanding the whole picture.

Throughout this book I have, thus, tried to give attention to those objective elements of the social reality that are often taken for granted because they are considered obvious and hence do not add much to the understanding of our realities. In this sense the study of worker mobilization may imply the following 'obvious' conditions: the pressure of the labour market and the lack of alternatives, the 'inevitability' of workers' dependency on a salary to earn a living and consequently their subordination within the employment contract, companies' repressive methods, ideologically dominant values produced by global competition, inequalities and a lack of access to social development. As far as worker mobilization is concerned all these factors are not old, or ideological but are simply conditions that we cannot avoid considering as immanent in the lives of the majority of workers and hence, to different extents, profoundly influencing opportunities for people to mobilize.

The attention to the micro contexts and to the dynamics of collective action has certainly produced a less detailed analysis of political processes and social mobilization external to the plants. In particular I refer to the way in which conflict has been politicized and how both workers and companies have reacted to this. What are the boundaries between workplace and social mobilization? What is the level of needs around which these two different instances of action are structured? Questions like these still remain unanswered. In the same line of criticism and with the same goals, more focused research could have offered deeper cultural accounts of the process of mobilization and the meaning of struggle.

Workplace resistance is a contested terrain, not just because it reproduces the never-ending debate between structure and agency in the construction of social reality, but also because it epitomizes the core contradictions existing within the capitalist mode of production and the unequal power relations on which the system is necessarily based. The cases presented in this book help to identify empirically some of these basic contradictions and power relations. On the one hand, workers are identified with the success of the companies but ignore the flexibility surrounding them; they know that they depend on an individual capital to survive and do whatever they can to contribute to the latter's success, but do not know how vain their efforts could be in a system based on competition. On the other hand, the dynamics of resistance described highlights the methods of direct repression or forced acceptance through which employers impose their command.

Workers do, however, struggle, resist and oppose despite these system-generated obstacles. In the case of FIAT, the workers' resistance was disruptive, action was direct and the occupation of the factory highly symbolic – solidarity and democracy constituted the workers' strengths. The experiences that the book has described are those of the struggle and resistance of particular groups of workers, in particular companies and in specific conditions. As such, the picture that it presents may or may not easily fit with other workers' realities. But especially when it comes to workers' resistance we should not be interested in generally applicable models. After all, the two principles that have greatly influenced any accounts of worker emancipation are those of the demystification of capital and praxis. This book is an attempt to contribute to both.

Notes on Methodology and the Fieldwork

The research on which this book is based started in October 2000 as a comparison of labour relations in two factories owned by the same multinational, FIAT, in Brazil and Argentina. The original idea was to look at the forms and methods of adaptation to new working practices used by trade unions and workers of the same company but within different industrial relations environments. The research seemed initially feasible as access to the plants for interviews and data collection was guaranteed by previously established relations with executives of the same enterprise. But as often happens to those who investigate sensitive business areas, the economic crisis of the company produced, together with worker redundancies and plant closures, a management decision to suspend any cooperation with researchers and, in my case, made it impossible to enter into the factories and develop the empirical part of the research.

During November 2001 and February 2002 I did the first field trip to Argentina and to the city of Córdoba as a sort of ritual way to put an end to my original research project, but also with the aim and hope of finding sufficient elements for a reformulation of it. I needed more details to explain why a modern plant inaugurated in 1997 and built to employ 5000 people and to produce 120,000 cars a year was, after less than four years, practically inactive. I was not certainly interested in researching how this happened. At the time of my visit to Córdoba, Italian newspapers in particular pointed to managerial mistakes and a short strategic vision of the enterprise as the causes of its lack of success. But in the plant closure there was something more important for a researcher in industrial relations. It was somehow essential to find an answer because the crash of FIAT in Argentina could also be seen as a confirmation that the paraphernalia of those practices labelled as human resource management (worker involvement, empowerment and participation) were, once again, more rhetoric than reality. At the same time, the failure of such managerial strategies, whose real effects both on increases in productivity and the individualization of employment relations were extensively criticized during the 1990s, was also bringing into question my approach to research. Was there any valid reason to look at industrial relations while continuing to insist on the analysis of the differences between workers' and unions' reactions to a managerially established agenda? Even from a perspective sympathetic with a 'new' model of labour relations based on reciprocal advantages for workers and companies, what happened at FIAT was the analysis of a failure.

The two factory occupations that took place in the FIAT Ferreyra's plant in September 1996 and January 1997 were certainly a surprise. I knew that the company had problems with its labour force in Argentina (trade unions have an old mentality the industrial relations director once said to me), but I could not imagine that a severe labour conflict was hidden behind the triumphalism that the inauguration of the new plant was receiving in both Argentina and Italy. In particular, by European standards, during the 1990s, factory occupations were almost a relic from the past. The search for more data on conflict in local newspapers revealed that another factory occupation had occurred in the city, in the CIADEA-Renault plant, at approximately the same time. I thus approached persons who could help me to establish further contacts with those who participated directly in the mobilizations and who were no longer working in the plants. My original research had changed completely and it had now become a comparison of worker mobilizations. It was an investigation into the causes that produced these mobilizations and into the social processes that took place among workers in such events. The plant closure and the decision of the company to suspend its cooperation with researchers, left me unexpectedly 'on the road', probably feeling the same emptiness, worries, fears and anger that are to a certain extent common, notwithstanding material differences, to all those who have just lost a job. The study of worker mobilizations became my own, almost natural, response to a passive and uncritical acceptance of the inevitability of the social system. The need to look at industrial relations as the study in which labour could be considered again as the central concern was, also because of my own experience, becoming urgent.

With this background in mind, which I am sure could be criticized as biased by any methodological purist, between November 2002 and February 2003, I did a second field trip to Córdoba and collected the bulk of the research's material. The majority of data came from in-depth, unstructured tape-recorded interviews with workers from both FIAT and CIADEA-Renault who had taken part in the events analysed and of people who, even if not directly involved, had a knowledge of the cases. The search for those workers who partici-pated in the factory occupations was time consuming because seven years after the events many of those employed by the two compan-ies had changed job, retired, migrated or lost contact with former co-workers. However people were always very supportive, both sad and proud of talking about the struggle they undertook, what was left of it and what went wrong.

The workers interviewed were very different. Indeed, I used a method of systematic diversification in order to get information: 'old' and 'new' workers, people in different departments and with differ-ent skills. At the same time, in the case of FIAT, a further important criteria for selection was represented by the level of involvement in the conflict, with three main groups of interviewees, equally repre-sented: people still in their jobs and presumably more loyal to the company, the activists and those in between.

The use of in-depth unstructured interviews proved to be the best instrument to achieve detailed accounts of the mobilizations analysed. In the workers' reconstructions of events, what happened was described as a whole, whose parts almost naturally seemed bent together, an automatic succession of actions and agents. Because of this, efforts to direct and fragment the interviews according to prede-fined theoretical categories would have been in vain and could have altered or confused the description of events. Thus the approach generally followed has been to leave the interviewees free to talk about the issues they considered more relevant, but guided through a number of selected area/hypothesis of research.

The first of these was concerned with a reconstruction of the dynamics of mobilization so as to identify internal and external fac-tors influencing the cases and a chronological sequence of the events.

The second was to see how, considering this specific dynamics, injustice was perceived and if it really represented the *conditio sine qua non* of collective action. The third wanted to investigate the role of solidarity in building collective action and thus aimed to discover the process of its formation. The fourth was to analyse issues of leadership and repression in collective action.

Another source of information was represented by newspapers articles relating to the time of the conflict and videos from the university TV channel. This was important as it offered, with the background and details of the cases, the possibility to compare this information with what was gathered from interviews and thus was very helpful in completing the puzzle of mobilizations.

Appendix: Extract from an Interview with the FIAT Workers' Elected Representative

Q: When did you get employed by FIAT?
A: In 1992.

Q: What was your job at that time?
A: I was a worker.

Q: A skilled worker?
A: No, no just a shop-floor worker. We were all employed at the same level independently of the level of study. When I did the interview they told me that my level of study was too high for the job, I was initially surprised by this but then I understood why ... the work you were asked to do was mechanical and repetitive, and maybe they needed somebody without much aspirations that to do that kind of job.

Q: Later on, with the new plant, they started to employ people with a better educational background?
A: No. They changed the profile of the workers they wanted to employ depending on the evolution of the struggle. Initially they hired people with a high level of education and these soon joined our struggle. Then they recruited people of 40–45 years old without educational background. We told them this was a mistake ... this kind of people were not used to the factory discipline, the quality decreased. Later on they changed again and recruited young people with primary level education from nearby shanty towns. But in many cases they had problems with thefts. So the composition of the workforce became very mixed and this created problems in production. It was a situation difficult to solve for them, which was entirely depending on the level and intensity of our struggle. They determined their workers' profile on the basis of the kind of people they did not want.

Q: And they did not want people like you ...
A: They did not want people who could have been easily convinced to join our struggle. In this our shop-floor delegates have been fundamental and because they were democratically elected had all the support from the workers.

Q: Between September 1996 and June 1997 there have been two factory occupations, can you describe these?
A: In the first one I did not participate, it did not occur during my shift and the day before I had resigned from FIAT. There were rumours about possible changes. The Italians were opening a new plants and we should have expected same changes. I personally thought these included salary cuts.

Q: It was the time of the reforms introducing labour flexibility?
A: The agreement between the government and FIAT opened the door to the introduction of labour flexibility, we were the first ... the day before the occupation they made all of us redundant but offered to be re-employed under a new agreement.

Q: What happened?
A: They called us individually into an office where the foremen, security guards and management were waiting. The new agreement was really bad, they reduced our salary from 4.80 to 2.80 pesos for an hour, reduced overtime payment, holidays. But the majority accepted because it was better than being unemployed and it was still possible to change your mind later on. For me the offer they made was far too low and I did not sign the new contract.

The day after the change to the new contract the guys went to the plant ... that night nobody slept. They went home, they calculated what they were going to receive, they discovered that they were going to earn half of their previous salary for doing the same job, they got depressed, they cried, they didn't sleep. The day after they reached the plant feeling bad, a collective bad feeling and without anybody suggesting anything to them, they got together.

Q: it was then a spontaneous decision?
A: Yes. What should we do? A guy, Daniel, with anger and fury for what happened shut violently one of the big factory gates and broke all the glass. Everybody looked at him and identified with him. Then he said 'let's occupy the factory' and people followed. This is

what people told me, I was not inside. I went to the plant just to get my last salary and payment but found out that the plant had been occupied.

Q: What was the company's attitude in this situation?
A: They did not know what to do, they were analysing the situation.

Q: And the internal security guards?
A: They did not do anything, the new contract was affecting also their salaries so the company had no idea with whom to establish a dialogue. Now I can say that this situation of uncertainty was very good for us, the company could not solve the problem quickly and people got together.

Q: What happened with Daniel?
A: He helped to create a new workers' commission. He looked for a lawyer and by chance the lawyer was a very good friend of mine ... and other comrades who were still outside with me pushed me inside the plant. There was a big assembly, everybody talking but with no direction. Once it came to my turn for speaking, I said what I thought it was necessary to do and that I was not directly interested anyway as I had already resigned. I just tried to put a bit of order. But people started to sing 'ole', ole', ole' Gallo, Gallo and after that I felt that I could not decide on my own, I could not move to Mendoza as I was planning to do, it was already a collective decision.

Q: Did you feel responsible?
A: Yes I felt this responsibility.

Q: Did the assembly then elected you in the commission?
A: Yes that's what happened. Later on the company tried to undermine this decision saying that because of my resignation I was not part of the workforce anymore and that I was thus not allowed to represent workers. But the assembly opposed this decision.

Q: What happened after the occupation ended?
A: The company accepted to negotiate with us, we got legal protection and support from the trade union that was formally representing us and through the government intervention we renegotiated the conditions of the work agreement, accepting a limited reduction of our salaries in exchange for the redundancy payment. This represented lots of money for the majority of workers many of whom had

more than ten years of seniority. Machines were also old and to get these working properly experienced workers were necessary and this was strategically important in the context of our struggle.

The company initially did not want to negotiate with us but they had to do it, partly because of the impossibility of running the plant without experienced workers and partly because we were really representing workers' interests. Later on to put pressure on the company, we took the decision not to train new workers because we knew that experience was our strength, but we always explained to the new why we were doing this.

Q: You told me that you were the first...
A: Yes but we started to reflect about this, about flexibility, Menem and the Argentina of convertibility once the occupation ended. We changed attitude, we started looking at our struggle in terms of class and the nine workers elected in the internal commission gained free movement within the plant.

Q: What was your role within the internal commission?
A: My comrades in the commission have always recognized the special relationship I had with the rest of the workers. So my opinion was always important but never imposed, we tried to establish a democratic exchange of ideas and decision-making process involving all the workers, both at the level of shop-floor delegates, a big group of 100 people approximately, and the general assembly.

Soon after the occupation ended, once we started to reflect upon the country we were living in and all the rest of it, we decided to build a stable organization. To strengthen this and to guarantee freedom to the internal commission it was decided in an assembly that the rest of the workers would pay them a salary.

Q: So the nine had no salary paid by the company?
A: No. Every day we moved from line to line listening to people's problems and getting organized for the months of December, January and February, when production is low. In these months the company do not desperately need workers and can provoke and put pressure on you. Thus during October and November we concentrated on organizing people by holding small assemblies of about 15 minutes in each line and shift. This was intended as a way to collect our comrades' complaints and thus with this pre-discussion establish

the most important issues to be discussed and voted at the general assembly. Every line grouped between 30 and 40 workers and thus these pre-discussions occupied an entire shift.

Q: What kind of issues were discussed?
A: We tried to concentrate primarily on issues of organization, we wanted to establish a plan for action and a strategy to get formal recognition as trade union. We discussed how to defend what we gained from our struggle, this was the most important thing for us. In doing this, we reconsidered our position in terms of politics and class. So we opposed the company's decision to invite Menem on the 20th of December for the inauguration of the new plant and threatened to demonstrate against this.

Q: This strategy was discussed among all of you?
A: This had been pre-discussed in all the assemblies, we all agreed on this. On that occasion we politicized our struggle because we were indicating Menem as the one responsible for labour flexibility. We discussed collectively that FIAT was the first but that later on the entire working class had to suffer the consequences of flexibility. So we knew that we were struggling not just to defend our own right but also those of other people and that we could have lost the struggle.

Q: Were you conscious of this?
A: We knew that we were going to lose.

Q: But nevertheless...
A: We had to struggle, we discussed about this in the assemblies.

Q: You discussed about the possibility of a failure?
A: Yes, but we decided to struggle and this was the most amazing thing.

Q: When did this happen?
A: I do not remember exactly but it was before the opening of the new plant. We used the three months after the first occupation to reach this conclusion. Why did we reach that level of discussion? Because after the occupation, as I told you before, we saw what was really going on around us. In that moment we had to stop the ball and think about where we were going. We knew that we were going to lose the struggle, we knew it.

Q: You were conscious that that you had to confront...

A: The provincial and national government, all the trade unions, the company...we never said that we were going to lose, of course nobody struggles if he doesn't see a possibility of winning, but we debated, and we voted in an assembly that losing was a possibility and that if we had lost the conflict they were going to fire all of us. And we had to opt and this was very important. We gave people the possibility of resigning. We looked around and we considered that resignation was one possibility and that the other was to struggle. If we wanted to struggle we had to do it well, if we wanted to resign as well. Nothing in the middle. In that situation resign meant bend your head [...] not just to accept Menem. Menem came together with other losses. The company was gradually trying to introduce new conditions, after the occupation it wanted to recover the space it had lost. We had to consider that fact.

Q: How did the company recover the space lost?

A: They tried to create contradictions between the internal commission and the workers, for instance circulating false information about our achievements during the negotiation meeting with management. They have always tried to break the relation between us and the rest of the workers.

Q: Who did this? The REPO?

A: They had many people doing this, REPO, foremen, psychologists working for the company, but mostly REPO were in charge of doing this, they were very fast.

Q: But people believed in the REPO?

A: No but there were small groups that tended to give more credit to them. These kinds of groups always exist and the REPO put pressure on them and worked to enlarge the group. Then in January, a member of the internal commission was fired.

Q: Was this for disciplinary reasons?

A: They were constantly provoking and they forced us to take extreme decisions. In this situation we realized that there was no other possibility than to maintain a high level of struggle. Meanwhile we had formally constituted a new trade union because this was democratically decided by all workers. Workers who were used to going home soon after the end of the working day, voted en masse. Management could not believe it. They video recorded all the assemblies even though these were always outside the factory gate and not during working time and then used these videos to put pressure on individual workers. It was really a persecution. But they could not do anything, at that time the level of mobilization, participation and consciousness was very high.

Q: How did you reach this stage?
A: Discussing, with lots of discussions and democracy.

Q: In the 25 years before these events, there was solidarity among workers, any form of resistance or opposition?
A: There was *compañerismo* and nothing else. That is why on the day of the factory occupation people were crying...I was crying, every half an hour I was crying. It was a situation for crying because solidarity, everything was unexpected, it was like something was set free, was released and this was positive for the people. It was positive not just in the economic sense but also as a way to feel realized as a person. They were feeling worthy persons and today everybody remembers that struggle and that they did well, well because they were feeling well. People were now different, the same person was not the same as before, he could see the world in a different way, he had 'jumped' and this happened to all of us, to all of us. The same struggle changed us, all of us, it changed us, it shaped us, it changed me and all of us. Emotion, I could say, in our case, was an essential element in our struggle.

Notes

1. Connected with my argument and worth mentioning, it is the question of whether Kelly's overreliance on social movements and social psychology theorists in the construction of the micro level of his mobilization theory could have represented an epistemological deviation from the overall genuine Marxist background of his theory. Ghigliani (2010) has focused on this aspect, by showing how the social movement and social psychology theorists' tendency to think about collective action as an aggregation of individualities may have left a 'birthmark' on Kelly's theory, particularly with his use of the concept of injustice and in his frequent references throughout Kelly (1998) to the construction of collective action as the sum of individual perceptions.
2. 'People are evidently inclined to grant legitimacy to anything that is or seems inevitable no matter how painful it may be. Otherwise the pain might be intolerable. The conquest of this sense of inevitability is essential to the development of politically effective moral outrage (injustice)' (Moore 1978, p. 459).
3. As Harvey (2006, p. 118) rightly argues, in a context such as that of the employment relationship that creates a structural unbalance in the power relations between the two parties, the voluntary nature of this cooperation is questionable.
4. The extracts from the interviews that are used in this and the following chapters have been left unchanged in their grammatical structure. Similarly, the translations provided have to be considered as a personal attempt to maintain unaltered the original discourse of the interviewees. 'la gente realmente opositora y que tenia peso o se fue, desapareció, lo mataron, no estuvieron mas. Lamentablemente los que quedamos a posteriori por cobardía, por necesidad, por la familia, por lo que quiera, nunca pudimos tener la fuerza, la capacidad, sì el disconformismo pero no la acción...estábavamos disconformes pero terminábamos haciendo los servicios y agachando la cabeza...ha pasado toda una generación intermedia que no ha tenido esos líderes con poder de hacer convocatorias de gente, con la opinión sólida que de ellos tenían los otros, entonces los nuevos que llegaron después de nosotros nos vieron continuando allí, pero como continuando? Haciendo siempre sí con la cabeza ...' (Renault white collar worker).
5. 'La misma Argentina esta' ya así el "no te metás", "vamos a luchar pero andá vos al frente", acá esta sociedad fue muy castigada en la época de los militares entonces es como que hay un miedo a exponerse. Viste lo que pasó en Bs. As. el año pasado a esta altura, que es cuando se armó la organización para el tema del corralito, reprimieron y mataron gente. Esa es la idea vieja que por el miedo quedó allí' (Renault production worker).

6. 'Siempre me mantuve con la capacidad de razonar que es lo que se le han quitado a la mayoría de la gente en estos años ... acá tenemos todavía recuerdo de lo que fue la dictadura militar y eso va a ser muy difícil cambiarlo ... acá no hay participación' (Fiat production worker).

7. The role of the CGTA (Confederación General de los Trabajadores Argentinos) was in this sense crucial. The centre was antagonistic to the traditional CGT (Confederación General del Trabajo) and offered, within its class and anti-bureaucratic discourse, a reference point for the establishment of workers' alliances in the city.

8. This name came from a speech by José Camilo Uriburu, Governor of Córdoba, who a few weeks before the uprising had promised to cut off the head of the poisonous snake (*vibora*) he considered the Córdoba labour movement at that time.

9. In Argentina, due to the political role trade unions have historically achieved, especially during authoritarian regimes, executives in power have commonly reduced unions' political and mobilization potential by both removing former leaders and substituting them with government functionaries and/or inhibiting through authority their normal functions of representation. This practice is known in Argentina as *intervención*, and English translations with the words intervention or union intervention do not explain properly what intervención means. This explicative note should clarify what frequently in the rest of the paper I mean by using the expression 'occupation, takeover by authority'.

10. This was a para-military organization created by José López Rega, former secretary of Perón and Ministry of Social Welfare in the government of Isabel Perón, who took the Presidency of Argentina after the death of Juan Domingo Perón in July 1974. López Rega represented the extreme right wing of the Peronist Movement and through the AAA he started a period of terror directed at the physical elimination of left wing and independent union leaders and political militants. The AAA severely hit Córdoba, where a Marxist oriented leadership of the labour movement, the so called *corriente clasista*, had emerged at the end of the 1960s.

11. The army commander of Córdoba, cynically, recognized the necessity to proceed with the killing of 50,000 people divided in order of priority between guerrilla and political activists, collaborators and a certain unavoidable number of 'mistakes'. Twenty-six years later these opinions were still seen as valid. While interviewing people in the FIAT plant I had an informal chat with one of the foremen. I provoked him by saying that I was desperately looking for an activist, a militant but that no one was left in the plant after the conflict, they really had done a good job. 'Yes', he said, 'we did like the military did, first the activists, than the less activist, then their friends, then the people who knew them and sometimes we also did some "mistakes".'

12. 'Al considerar el período 1976/1979 debe tenerse presente esta terrible hipoteca que pesaba sobre cualquier conflicto laboral: el trabajador que desafiaba la soberanía patronal en un aspecto mínimo o en uno decisivo, arriesgaba, cuando menos, su empleo y, con frecuencia, su libertad, su

seguridad y su propia vida ... la persecución ideológica fue otra de las constantes de este periodo. El trabajador que tuviera antecedentes políticos o sindicales era catalogado inmediatamente de subversivo y ello lo descalificaba para ingresar' (Abós 1984, p. 44).

13. In a first report commissioned by the US government, the Vance commission (1976–78) reported that 20 per cent of physical disappearances were of workers or trade unionists. Gallittelli and Thompson (1982) argue that this percentage of workers probably increased after 1978 because by then the guerrilla organizations were already destroyed while the total number of people disappeared amounted to 30,000 at the end of the dictatorship.

14. Recent decisions of the Supreme Court on workers' right of association and of the Ministry of Labour on the '*de facto*' recognition of the Buenos Aires's underground's workers' independent trade union, seem to, however, indicate a counter-tendency.

15. During the last years of Perón, foreign investments were promoted in new industrial areas of the country. Particular emphasis was put on the attraction of those products, like motor vehicles, which were more technologically innovative.

16. This is the case of SMATA Córdoba, for instance, where the same secretary had been in power since 1976.

17. 'Para nosotros, la vuelta de Perón era la vuelta de la decencia y la dignidad para los que trabajamos, sacarnos la pata del patrón de encima, era la vuelta de la felicidad, era el final de tanta tristeza y tanta amargura que había en los millones de hombres del pueblo, era el fin de la persecución ...' (James 1990, p. 128).

18. 'El sindicalista debe luchar con todas sus convicciones, todas sus fuerzas para cambiar el sistema. El dirigente sindical debe saber que pese a una "buena economía" si no hay una justa distribución de la riqueza la explotación prosigue. Y por lo tanto debe luchar por la liberación social. El dirigente debe saber que jamás habrá buenos convenios de trabajo con una economía del país supeditada a los monopolios. Y por lo tanto debe luchar por la liberación nacional' (in James 1990, p. 307).

19. It is interesting to note the similarities between Córdoba and the Córdobazo and that of Turin, in approximately the same period, during the so called 'Hot Autumn'. In both cases we have young migrant workers, living in new neighbourhoods near the plants and who were having their first experience of work in a car factory. These common backgrounds, among other factors, certainly produced a class-conscious identity and the potential for rebellion and radicalization. In the case of FIAT/Turin, in particular, the change of production system and working patterns that occurred at that time contributed to unifying the demands of the 'old' skilled workers with those of the 'new' unskilled migrants. See Castronovo (1999) and, for a militant perspective, Balestrini (1977).

20. It was not uncommon to work in a factory and study part-time.

21. '... cambio' totalmente la vida en la fabrica. Los delegados nos defendían de los jefes frente a todos los problemas que surgían en el trabajo, controlamos los ritmos de producción que antes eran terribles. En fin,

eliminamos el clima opresivo que se vivía en la fabrica y pudimos reivindicar nuestros derechos como seres humanos' (in James 1990, p. 306).
22. '...significa que los que tenemos trabajo estamos cediendo un pedacito de empleo para que otro lo tenga o que lo cedemos para no recuperarlo nunca más y que nada ocurra?' (*La Voz del Interior*, 12 October 1996).
23. In its original version: 'il sindacato è obiettivamente nient'altro che una società commerciale, di tipo prettamente capitalistico, la quale tende a realizzare, nell'interesse del proletariato, un prezzo massimo per la merce-lavoro e a realizzare il monopolio di questa merce nel campo nazionale e internazionale' ('Le masse e i capi', Ordine Nuovo 30 Ottobre 1921) in Gramsci 1969, pp. 501–504.
24. SITRAMF is the acronym for Sindicato de Trabajadores Mecánicos de Ferreyra. The name voluntarily recalled the anti-bureaucratic experience and the militancy of the historic *clasista* union SITRAC.
25. *Fabbrica integrata* can be approximately understood as a model of lean production and 'just in time'. The name, in particular, comes from the fact that suppliers operate in the same industrial area and provide the parts to be assembled directly to the lines.
26. 'Mirá acá se mueve la gente de esta forma: si hay una asamblea métete en el medio, ni salgas primero ni salgas último que vos sos nuevo y no te quedes. O sea, ellos mismos te decían que te fueras de irte y de no quedarte para hacer buena letra con el sindicato' (Fiat production worker).
27. Make or create troubles.
28. 'El gremio está vendido, nos echó más que la fábrica'; 'están disfrazados de corderos pero son lobos' (Renault maintenance worker); 'después te podría hablar del gremio pero no se' en que te sirve...no confiamos mucho en el gremio, son todos unos vendidos'; 'el gremio por un lado nos defendía y por el otro nos pisaba la cabeza' (Renault production worker); 'el sindicato es connivente y perpetuo en el poder' 'es como una mafia, ni más ni menos'; 'La misma gente que estaba en el gremio con los militares sigue en la dirigencia del sindicato, es la mafia' (Renault production worker).
29. In 1998 the company also participated in a European sponsored project on trade union/company committees for participation and joint training.
30. It should also be noted that FIAT represents a pattern-setting outstanding case rather than a model representative of Italian industrial relations.
31. 'Nosotros dentro de FIAT gozábamos de un verano, no así los trabajadores de la siderurgia, y de esto la gente no se daba cuenta, como uno que queda en su isla...no quiere que se la muevan' (Fiat worker formerly employed in the casting sector).
32. 'FIAT cierra el nuevo convenio con SMATA. Teníamos una planta que tenia que pasar a una nueva empresa con condiciones salariales inferiores a las que tenían...era muy difícil' (FIAT, former REPO).
33. 'El día del pase era un día secreto, se sorprendió a la planta, a todo el mundo' (FIAT, former REPO).
34. Under Argentine law, workers, when a company ceases to exist, are entitled to receive a sum of money that is calculated on the basis of one month's salary per year of employment.

35. 'Vos entrabas un día, te agarraban y el jefe te decía de no prender la
    máquina de andar a hablar con el REPO y el tipo estaba con tu renuncia
    y tu nuevo contracto y vos tenías que firmar con un guardia parado al
    costado. Si vos decías que lo quería pensar no te daban tiempo, o estabas
    o te ibas. Muchos en esa situación firmaron pensando que después las
    cosas se podían cambiar y otros no aceptaron desde el principio y se
    fueron. Si vos vas a tu trabajo que todos los días ha sido igual y de un día
    para otro te dicen que tenés que renunciar y que te bajan el salario de un
    50 % y que si no te despiden... te agarra frío, no tenés otras perspectivas,
    no tenés tiempo ni de pensar en otro trabajo o de invertir la plata en otra
    cosa' (FIAT worker).
36. 'El odio fue a los dos. Una fue la toma en contra de la fabrica, la otra
    fue la de ir a las casas de los delegados para reventarlos, romperle la
    casa, no quedo' uno, desaparecieron esa noche de Córdoba... normal-
    mente la burocracia nos pone miedo a nosotros, nos pega a nosotros,
    esta vez fue al revés' (FIAT activist).
37. 'Si', todos la teníamos (la camiseta). Si a mi me decían, "hace esto", yo lo
    hacía, cumplía con las cosas de mi trabajo, estábamos muy a gusto con
    esto, teníamos interés en que se produjera' (Fiat worker).
38. 'la empresa toma otra postura que no es solo la producción si no como
    involucra la familia del trabajador en el proceso productivo, en la grande
    familia FIAT. Hacíamos fiestas de cumpleaños para todos los chicos, rega-
    los para Navidad, ano Nuevo, ... un involucramiento total no solamente
    productivo, ideológico, para mí fue terrible porque yo veía al revés todo
    lo que era y me sentía muy solo' (FIAT activist).
39. 'Me rompió todo un proyecto de vida, me destruyó a mi y a mi familia,
    yo no podía aceptar esa idea' (member of the independent union com-
    mission); 'Te sentías estafado, es como cuando a un chico le compras un
    juguete y cuando se lo estás por dar, el chico con toda la ilusión de jugar,
    le decís "no era para vos era para el otro"' (independent union dele-
    gate); 'En esa fábrica siempre se trabajó mucho, los ritmos de producción
    eran elevados. La gente trabajaba mucho y estaba orgullosa de trabajar
    por esa empresa. Ellos no quisieron reconocer eso y la gente se sintió
    traicionada y bueno si entonces no tengo ningún valor yo me siento
    agredido' (FIAT workers' elected representative).
40. 'uno es realista, siempre esta' del lado de la empresa. En todo aspecto uno
    tiene que ser conciente que una empresa paga el sueldo por el trabajo que
    uno hace y vos tenes que estar de acuerdo con ese trabajo. Yo siempre
    estuve de ese lado, si no me gusta me voy. Si yo en ese momento estaba
    detrás de la maquina haciendo lo mismo y ganando meno no te podría
    decir lo que hubiera hecho' (FIAT REPO, former production worker).
41. 'Yo tengo una familia, no es cuestión de decir: "bueno me voy", si después
    no tengo nada. No es que estoy yo solo, atrás mío hay un grupo de gente.
    Lamentablemente es así' (FIAT worker).
42. 'Lo que pasa es que esa gente que tiene prácticamente una vida allí adentro
    de esa fábrica a lo mejor no ve las cosas como uno pensando que se iba de la
    fábrica. Un tipo que vivió allí adentro, sale de una fábrica a la calle a buscar

trabajo y no sabe que hacer, no sabe vender nada porque el ordenó su vida trabajando allí y si vos lo mandás en la esquina a vender un mantecol no sabe como hacerlo' (member of the independent union commission).
43. 'Al otro día entramos y fue una cosa rarísima. Yo entraba más tarde, el área de calidad entraba mas tarde, y teníamos que pasar por toda la planta, un ambiente raro... la gente reunida en todos los rinconcitos, todo el mundo reunido, era como que el día no arrancaba... llegamos al vestuario pero ni nos cambiamos, "che, ahí dice un muchacho que hay que juntarnos" y todo el mundo, fue una cosa instantánea. Vamos para adelante, a la placita que está frente a la planta, los delegados ninguno, nadie estaba, esto no es lo que se nos dijo... alguien que explique... que es lo que habían dicho a todo el mundo no solo a mi... vamos a pedir explicaciones, vamos a pedir explicaciones. Y la gente ordenada salió, yo creo que no faltó nadie y fueron caminando para adelante "che, que pasa?"' (FIAT worker, Quality Control Department).
44. 'Estábamos perdidos, no teníamos rumbo, nos habían pegado fuerte, tan fuerte que nos enloqueció, llegó' un momento que no pensábamos, la gente no quería creer pero estaba dispuesta a cualquier cosa' (member of the independent union commission).
45. 'Los viejos teníamos tal vez mas espíritu de lucha porque veíamos la injusticia después de tantos anos de trabajar. Sentíamos que nos habían marginados, que ya no valíamos nada' (FIAT 'old' worker).
46. 'Fuimos al choque de entrada y no era pero te obligaban porque tampoco había otra salida, te obligaban a dar ese choque. Al hacerlo tan compulsivo y tan drástica la rebaja de sueldo fue un golpe duro y tenías que responderlo con otro golpe duro no había otra' (FIAT worker).
47. 'fue un golpe muy fuerte y en muy poco tiempo. Por allí si nos hubiéramos encontrado en la situación de la Renault que se vino más gradualmente... pero en el caso de nosotros no. Nos quebraron en el medio, no nos fueron disolviendo, directamente nos pegaron un golpe y nos partieron en la mitad' (delegate of the independent union).
48. 'Una charla político gremial tanto del gremio como de la empresa que de alguna forma arreglaron, en este sentido siempre salimos perjudicados los operarios' (Renault worker).
49. 'El pensamiento sindical era de no mezclarte con los problemas de los otros,' 'vos métete en lo tuyo y nada más y quien se jodió, se jodió' (Renault worker).
50. 'Muchos comentan que, en realidad, el gremio y la empresa arreglan y a la gente le dicen otras cosas. Pero aparentemente es así porque no se consiguió nada. Nos sentíamos impotentes y tampoco podíamos buscar otra salida con otros representantes, el gremio te lo impedía' (Renault worker).
51. 'Todos somos concientes, todos... lamentablemente por dentro cuantas broncas hemos tenido? Pero miles y broncas, broncas. Te lo tenes que aguantar por la familia, tenés que aguantar muchas cosas' (Renault worker).
52. 'La solidaridad siempre existe, es espontánea. Lo que pasa es que la represión, hoy son las leyes de trabajo flexible ayer era más el ejercito, y la falta de organización la rompen' (SITRAC's activist).

53. 'la gente no era tan solidaria ... (por) el hecho de tener un buen sueldo o una situación cómoda adentro del ambiente obrero nacional, nadie quería perder nada. La gente que estaba metida en esta historia, viste, entonces se ponía,... perdía de vista unos intereses comunes' (FIAT worker Quality Control Department).

54. 'En Cormec no había razones para el conflicto y tampoco había políticas sindicales, las asambleas que se hacían eran por boludeses te sentabas allí para fumarte un faso ...' (FIAT worker).

55. ''había alta producción en primer lugar, había horas extras, necesitaban a los trabajadores porque era época record en la producción automotor de la Argentina, en crecimiento continuo y fuerte y de exportación hacía Brasil. Eso significaba que los trabajadores trabajaban un tercer turno para satisfacer esa fuerte demanda. Por lo tanto no había presión por parte de la fabrica, mas bien tentaba cumplir siempre con las reglas del convenio que teníamos' (FIAT activist).

56. 'en ese entonces todo estaba tranquilo, se ganaba bien y el resto no importaba. Siempre se hacían fiestas, siempre había gente por eso pero no para la lucha' (FIAT activist).

57. 'Un poco cansados y al final perdimos de vista los objetivos que teníamos nosotros como trabajadores. Todo estaba dado o iba dándose. Recién se iba incorporando en el 83 la gente a la democracia a la libertad, estábamos todavía en un momento de transición. No había muchas cosas para pelear ...' (FIAT worker, Quality Control Department).

58. 'los nuevos no tuvieron ejemplos porque' lo único que encontraron fue un montón de gente agachando la cabeza y diciendo sí señor, sí señor' (Renault worker).

59. 'Siempre la política de la empresa ha sido la de dividirnos y de separarnos si tenía sospecha de que nos podíamos agrupar y ser solidarios entre nosotros. Trataban de crear discordia ... te vuelvo a repetir que el perjudicado siempre es el operario, no sé si por falta de actividad nuestra o por cálculo de ellos' (Renault worker).

60. 'la empresa contribuyó en romper la solidaridad, yo creo. Ese fue o es donde mas apunta la fabrica, a romper la unión entre los compañeros, lo hemos vivido allí adentro, estoy seguro' (Renault worker).

61. 'Lo que había era compañerismo y nada más. Por eso la gente el día de la toma lloraba ... yo lloraba, cada media hora estaba llorando. Era para llorar porque la solidaridad, todo esto nació de golpe, fue como algo que se liberó y eso le hacía bien a la gente. Ya no bien en el sentido económico, bien en el sentido de realizarse como persona. Se sentían dignos y hoy cualquier persona se acuerda de esa lucha y que hizo bien, porque se sintió bien' (FIAT workers' elected representative).

62. 'No sólo nos redujeron el sueldo, fue compulsivo, fue un arreglo entre todos: Gobiernos, sindicatos, patronal, todos juntos ... en ese momento, te digo lo que fue para mí, me daba y todavía me da vergüenza venir a decirle a mi familia que yo no la iba a poder mantener. Yo de un sueldo pasaba a ganar la mitad con muchas condiciones esclavizantes y sin haber levantado un dedo ... pienso que todos nosotros podemos reaccionar

muy, muy violentemente cuando te tocan algo que querés mucho más que a vos y que no tenía otra posibilidad' (FIAT maintenance worker).

63. 'Me sentí engañado y en ese momento se me rompió la relación con la fábrica' (FIAT Quality Control Department).

64. 'La gente se sintió traicionada por el gremio y defraudada y abandonada por la empresa' (CPI FIAT).

65. 'Vivías como un pollo para el matadero: ibas a trabajar, comías de tu platito, te engordaban y al asador. Era así. Después te mostraron que te iban a engordar meno, te achicamos la jaula, te sacamos mucha agua de la comida pero de toda forma vas al matadero' (FIAT activist).

66. 'Acá la fábrica no te echa, te suspende, te va ahogando, ahogando hasta que vos decís "bueno acá me están ahorcando". Pero nunca echó a nadie, te suspenden. Ellos no tienen apuro, el que tiene apuro sos vos que tenés cuentas para pagar y no podés' (Renault worker).

67. 'Estabas rodeado sin poder arrancar, te tenías que quedar en el medio. Eso es lo que pasó. Todos tenían miedo a perder el trabajo, miedo al Gobierno, a la fábrica, al sindicato. Miedo, miedo, miedo y los viejos que estaban de antes arreglaban con la fábrica y chau' (Renault worker).

68. 'Se estableció un debate, era todo un debate en la planta. Después de eso se comienza todo un movimiento, empiezan a movilizarse. No sabían bien para donde ir ni que hacer pero empiezan a juntarse, era mucha gente y comienza una movilización interna de fábrica sin líderes que la siguieran. Cuando se da esta situación ya en la propia movilización comienzan a aparecer los líderes naturales, propios, la gente de más carácter, más tamaño, el más malo, el que levantaba a voz y decía vamos. Ese que decía vamos era lo que encaminaba la movilización. Empiezan a perfilarse algunos representantes espontáneos, naturales' (FIAT, former REPO).

69. 'El día de la firma la actitud de rebeldía fue no trabajar, la gente estaba pensando, era una cosa terrible, charlar, charlar para ver lo que se hacia' (FIAT's activist).

70. 'Al otro día los muchachos entraron en la fabrica...esa noche no durmió nadie. Se fueron a sus casas, hicieron las cuentas, se dieron cuenta que iban a ganar la mitad de la plata por el mismo trabajo. Se deprimieron, lloraron, no durmieron. Al otro día llegaron mal, colectivamente mal a la fábrica y sin que nadie les dijera nada se juntaron. Que hacemos?' (FIAT workers' elected representative).

71. 'Ese día estábamos conversando al y hubo un momento en que llegó un silencio... porque fue generalizado el sentimiento y a mi me agarró nervios Vos sabés que yo en ese momento.... había una tablera de la máquina que yo empecé' a pegar de puños, no me dolía, por sacarme la bronca. Pasa el jefe en ese momento y me ve y en esos momentos toda la gente a mi me seguía y los demás también empezaron a golpear y así todas las líneas. Donde probaban los motores a los motores empezaron a sacarle los silenciadores, más yo golpeaba más los demás me seguían' (FIAT's independent union delegate).

72. 'Me levanté y le di vuelta a la mesa y le dije "acá nosotros vamos a hacer lo que la masa decida y si la masa decide no trabajar, no vamos a

trabajar, está?". "Ustedes no son nada". "Si somos muchos, somos trabajadores". "Vos de esta manera no me hablás, soy tu jefe!". "Vos ahora no sos nada y yo me voy a levantar y me voy a ir afuera y quien me quiera seguir que me siga'" (FIAT's independent union delegate).

73. 'Ellos pensaban que yo era maravilloso como líder porque' había logrado de transformar esa masa de corderos con la camiseta puesta en luchadores ejemplares. Pero fueron ellos a lograrlo!! Ellos lo lograron. Lo único que yo hice fue de explicitar esa situación nada más' (FIAT workers' elected representative).

74. 'Yo sé que en esos momentos hubo una tirada de bronca, le llamó la atención a la gente de personal porque no estaba esa persona en otro lado y no en contra de la empresa' (former CPI FIAT).

75. 'En la segunda toma con el activismo tomando un papel protagónico se rompe al vínculo democrático con la base, eso fue un error. Muchas veces el activismo toma en sus manos el veneno que cada uno tiene encima' (independent union member).

76. 'Después de la toma conocí a otro tipo de gente con la cual llegamos a la política...antes éramos una isla' (Fiat worker, Quality Control Department).

77. 'Aumentaban los temores de que el conflicto se extendiera a otras plantas y que frente a la ex Cormec se realizara el acto central de la protesta del Jueves' (*La Voz del Interior*, 24 September 1996).

78. 'Yo no me olvidaré nunca cuando Gallo decía: "hemos recuperado el poder de decisión nuestro, de tomar decisiones." Nosotros recuperamos el poder de lucha, de discusión, antes no se discutía nada. Y era tan fuerte el grupo...era lindo' (FIAT worker production line, La Morenita).

79. 'La gente empezó a identificarse muchísimo con los equipos de trabajo y se recuperó ó la planta. Los voceros fueron abandonados y se empezaron a ir...los echamos' (FIAT, former REPO).

80. 'Imposible recuperar a la gente. Se tubo que ir mucha gente que no había posibilidad de que volviera a identificarse con el compromiso. Fueron despedidos se fueron solos' (FIAT, former REPO).

81. 'Nosotros sentimos, y realmente era así, que estábamos solos, fuimos los primeros' (independent union delegate).

82. 'Vos ibas y le avisabas a los vagos "che loco, les van a bajar el sueldo" y los tipos "no, no creo". Hasta que no te tocan no te metes. En la Chevrolet lo hacían salir de la puerta trasera y ninguno se acercó a nosotros' (FIAT worker, Quality Control Department).

83. 'la fábrica no nos podía manejar. Cualquier cosa era batucada, golpear la máquina, se hacia batucada por cualquier cosa. La voluntad de la gente no era la misma. Los viejos que estaban acostumbrado a poner a punto las máquinas ya no lo hacían más por esa plata. La gente se fue haciendo rebelde' (FIAT worker).

84. 'La planta era realmente un desmanejo, no se tenía control, tal como te digo, el operario hacia lo que quería, trabajaba como quería y esta gente tenía realmente toda la sensación de la gente, porque la gente estaba realmente enojada. No que los querían a estos nueves? si no que estaban enojados y lo representaban de esta forma' (FIAT, former REPO).

85. 'Cuando se tomó la fábrica por primera vez, no teníamos mucha conciencia de los que estábamos haciendo' (FIAT worker, production line La Morenita).
86. 'ahora habían cambiado, esa misma persona ya no era la de antes, ya veía el mundo diferente, había pegado un salto y esto le sucedió a todos, a todos. La lucha misma nos cambio' a todos, nos fue cambiando, modelando, a mí y a todos. Entonces lo emotivo en lo nuestro yo te diría fue un elemento esencial en nuestra lucha' (FIAT workers' elected representative).
87. 'Éramos parte de eso, estábamos en el medio de eso. Vos sabes que nosotros empezamos en ese momento a darnos cuenta de todo lo que era la flexibilización y de todo lo que iba a venir en el país' (FIAT worker Quality Control Department).
88. 'hubo en todo el proceso que duro' un año, un año y medio una toma de conciencia muy grande por parte de todos, independientemente de la posición que asumieron en los momentos de lucha' (FIAT worker, production line).
89. 'la empresa nunca los reconoció legalmente, siempre se los trató como un hecho concreto, una representación de hecho, es decir si es con ustedes que tengo que hablar, hablo pero no les voy a reconocer ningún carácter sindical. Para nosotros el sindicato era SMATA' (FIAT, former REPO).
90. 'En ningún momento nosotros dijimos vamos a perder, por supuesto nadie pelea si no tiene alguna posibilidad de ganar pero nosotros discutimos y votamos en asamblea que había posibilidad de perder y que si perdíamos nos iban a despedir a todos. Y que teníamos que optar, esto fue muy importante. Dimos a la gente la posibilidad de resignar. Nos miramos alrededor y nos dimos cuenta que la resignación era una posibilidad y la otra era pelear. Si peleamos bien y si resignamos bien. A media no. En esos términos, resignar significaba agachar la cabeza... no solamente que venga Menem eso seria lo de meno. Que venga Menem traía emparejado la perdida de otras cosas. La empresa de a poco te quería meter imposiciones, pasada la toma de a poco quería recuperar terreno. Y ese recuperar terreno nosotros lo teníamos que tener en cuenta' (FIAT workers' elected representative).
91. 'los mismos jefes me decían activista y yo les decía, porque activista? Para decir la verdad? Para pelear, para reclamar lo que es justo? Ellos trataban de aplastarte, de que vos renunciara. Me llamaron muchas veces, yo no quise renunciar hasta que me despidieron' (FIAT worker, La Morenita).
92. 'Los jefes te decían que te habían visto hablar con los muchachos del sindicato y que esto te iba a dar problemas, que era mejor dejar de hacer esto' (FIAT workers' elected representative and FIAT worker, La Morenita).
93. 'I licenziamenti degli attivisti più facinorosi hanno avuto carattere simbolico e segnato la riaffermazione dell'ordine interno e delle prerogative manageriali' (Camuffo and Massone 2001, p. 68).
94. Those who were fired after the second occupation built a tent in front of the plant to receive solidarity from other colleagues and to maintain links with those inside the plant.

Bibliography

Abós, A. (1984), Las organizaciones sindicales y el poder militar (1976–1983), *Biblioteca Política Argentina*, Buenos Aires: Centro Editor de América Latina.

Almond, P. and Ferner, A. (eds) (2006), *American Multinationals in Europe: Managing Employment Relations across National Borders*, Oxford: Oxford University Press.

Atzeni, M. (2009), Searching for injustice and finding solidarity? A contribution to the mobilization theory debate, *Industrial Relations Journal*, 40(1): 5–16.

Atzeni, M. and Ghigliani, P. (2009), Labour movement in Argentina since 1945: The limits of trade union reformism, in *Trade Unionism since 1945: Toward a Global History, Volume 2: The Americas, Asia and Australia*, edited by C. Phelan, 223–248, Oxford: Peter Lang.

Atzeni, M. and Ghigliani, P. (2007a), Labour process and decision-making in factories under workers' self-management: empirical evidence from Argentina. *Work, Employment and Society*, 21(4): 653–672.

Atzeni, M. and Ghigliani, P. (2007b), The resilience of traditional trade union practices in the revitalisation of the Argentine labour movement, in '*Trade Union Revitalisation: Trends and Prospects in 34 Nations*', edited by C. Phelan, Oxford: Peter Lang.

Balestrini, N. (1977), *Vogliamo tutto*, Milano: Feltrinelli.

Battistini, O. and Montes Cató, J. (2000), Flexibilización laboral en Argentina, un camino hacia la precarización y la desocupación, *Revista Venezolana de Gerencia*, 5(10), 63–89.

Beynon, H. (1984), *Working for Ford*, London: Penguin.

Bonazzi, G. (1994), A gentler way to total quality? The case of the 'integrated factory' at FIAT Auto, in Elgar, T. and Smith, C. eds, *Global Japanisation? The Transnational Transformation of the Labour Process*, London: Routledge.

Brennan, J.P. (1994), *The Labour Wars in Córdoba, 1955/1976. Ideology, Work and Labour Politics in an Argentine Industrial City*, Cambridge, MA and London: Harvard University Press.

Brown Johnson, N. and Jarley, P. (2004), Justice and union participation: an extension and test of mobilization theory. *British Journal of Industrial Relations*, 42: 543–562.

Bruno, R. (1999), *Steelworkers Alley: How Class Works in Youngstown*, Ithaca, NY: ILR Press.

Burawoy, M. (1979), *Manufacturing Consent, Changes in the Labour Process under Monopoly Capitalism*, Chicago: University of Chicago Press.

Camuffo, A. and Massone, L. (2001), Relazioni Industriali e Globalizzazione: la strategia di FIAT Auto, *Economia & Management*, 1, Gennaio 2001, 55–74.

Camuffo, A. and Volpato, G. (1995), The labour relations heritage and lean manufacturing at FIAT Auto, *International Journal of Human Resource Management*, 6(4), 795–824.

Cangiano, M.C. (1998), Reviewing the past and inventing the present: the steelworkers of Villa Constitución and Menemismo, in *Peronism and Argentina*, edited by Brennan, J.P., Wilmington: SR Books.

Castronovo, V. (1999), *FIAT 1899–1999: un secolo di storia italiana*, Milano: RCS Libri.

Cohen, S. (2006), *Ramparts of Resistance, Why Workers Lost Their Power and How to Get It Back*, London: Pluto.

Cohen, S. (1987), A labour process to nowhere, *New Left Review*, I/165, available at http://www.newleftreview.org/?view=299.

Corradi, J.E. (1987), The culture of fear in civil society, in Peralta-Ramos, M. and Waisman, C.H. eds, *From Military Rule to Liberal Democracy in Argentina*, Westview Special Studies on Latin America and the Caribbean, Boulder, CO and London: Westview Press.

Cox, A., Sung, S., Hebson, G. and Oliver, G. (2007), Applying union mobilization theory to explain gendered collective grievances: Two UK case studies, *Journal of Industrial Relations*, Industrial Relations Society of Australia, 49(5): 717–739.

Darlington, R. (2007), Leadership and union militancy: the case of the RMT, paper presented at, *International Industrial Relations Association Conference*, 3–6 September 2007, University of Manchester.

Darlington, R. (2002), Shop stewards' leadership, left-wing activism and collective workplace union organisation, *Capital and Class*, 76: 95–126.

Darlington, R. (2001), Union militancy and left-wing leadership on London underground, *Industrial Relations Journal*, 32: 2–21.

Darlington, R. (1994), *The Dynamics of Workplace Unionism: Shop Stewards Organisation in Three Merseyside Plants*, London: Mansell.

Delich, F. (1970), *Crisis y protesta social. Córdoba Mayo de 1969*, Buenos Aires: Signos.

Dinerstein, A.C. (2001a), *The violence of stability: an investigation of the subjectivity of labour in Argentina*, PhD Thesis, University of Warwick, Department of Sociology.

Dinerstein, A.C. (2001b), Roadblocks: against the violence of stability, *Capital and Class*, 74: 1–7.

Duval, N. (2001), *Los sindicatos clasistas: SITRAC (1970–1971)*, Córdoba, Argentina: Fundación Pedro Milesi, Biblioteca Popular de Bella Vista.

Edwards, P.K. (1986), *Conflict at Work*, Oxford: Blackwell.

Edwards, P.K. and Scullion, H. (1982), *The Social Organisation of Industrial Conflict*, Oxford: Blackwell.

Ellis, J. (2004), More than a token gesture: NGOs and trade unions campaigning for a common cause, *Development in Practice*, 14: 248–253.

Evangelista, L. (1998), *Voices of the Survivors: Testimony, Mourning and Memory in Post-Dictatorship Argentina (1983–1995)*, New York, London: Garland Publishing, Latin America Studies.

Fairbrother, P. (2005), Review of Gall, G. (2003). *Union Organising: Campaigning for Trade Unions Recognition, London: Routledge. Capital and Class*, 87: 257–263.

Falcón, R. (1982), Conflicto Social y Régimen Militar. La resistencia obrera en Argentina (Marzo 1976–Marzo 1981), in Gallittelli, B. and Thompson, A. eds (1982), *Sindicalismo y regimenes militares en Argentina y Chile*, Amsterdam: Cedla Publications, Cedla.

Fantasia, R. (1995), From class consciousness to culture, action and social organisation, *Annual Review of Sociology*, 21: 269–287.

Fantasia, R. (1988), *Cultures of Solidarity: Consciousness, Action and Contemporary American Workers*, Berkeley: University of California Press.

Fernández, A. (1997), *Flexibilización laboral y crisis del sindicalismo*, Buenos Aires: Espacio.

Fernández, A. (1998), *Crisis y decadencia del Sindicalismo Argentino: sus causas sociales y políticas*, Buenos Aires: Editores de America Latina.

Franzosi, R. (1995), *The Puzzle of Strikes*, Cambridge: Cambridge University Press.

Gall, G. (2003), *Union Organising: Campaigning for Trade Unions Recognition*, London: Routledge.

Gall, G. (2000a), Debating mobilization, class struggle and the left: a response to a replay, *Historical Materialism*, 7(1): 175–180.

Gall, G. (2000b), New technology, the labour process and employment relations in the provincial newspapers industry, *New Technology, Work and Employment*, 15(2): 94–107.

Gall, G. (1999), What is to be done with organised labour? *Historical Materialism*, 5: 327–343.

Gallittelli, B. and Thompson, A. (eds) (1982), *Sindicalismo y regimenes militares en Argentina y Chile*, Amsterdam: Cedla Publications, Cedla.

Ghigliani, P. (2005), International trade unionism in a globalizing world: a case study of new labour internationalism, *Economic and Industrial Democracy*, 26(3): 359–382.

Ghigliani, P. (2010), *The Politics of Privatisation and Trade Union Mobilisation: The Electricity Industry in UK and Argentina*, Peter Lang: Oxford.

Ghigliani, P. and Flier, P. (1999), Acme and decadence of the labour reforming movement in Argentina: the syndical movement and the policies of social security. By way of balance, paper presented at the *35th Conference of ITH. The 20th Century of the Labour Movement*, Linz 15/18 September 1999.

Godio, J. (2000), *Historia del movimiento obrero argentino (1870–2000)*, Vol. 2, La época de hegemonía del sindicalismo Peronista 1943–2000, Buenos Aires: Corregidor.

Gordillo, M. (1999), *Córdoba en los 60', la experiencia del sindicalismo combativo*, Córdoba, Argentina: Universidad Nacional de Córdoba.

Gramsci, A. (1991), *Quaderni del carcere: note sul Macchiavelli, sulla politica e sullo stato moderno*, Roma: Editori Riuniti.

Gramsci, A. (1969), *Scritti Politici*, Roma: Editori Riuniti.

Green, A.M., Black, J. and Ackers, P. (2000), The union makes us strong? A study of the dynamics of workplace union leadership at two UK manufacturing plants, *British Journal of Industrial Relations*, 38: 75–93.

Green, P. (1990), *The Enemy Without: Policing and Class Consciousness in the Miners' Strike*, New directions in Criminology series, Milton Keynes: Open University Press.

Hanagan, M. (1980), *The Logic of Solidarity: Artisans and Industrial Workers in Three French Towns, 1871–1914*, Urbana: University of Illinois Press.

Harvey, D. (2006), *The Limits to Capital*, London: Verso.

Heery, E. (2002), Partnership versus organising: alternative futures for British trade unionism, *Industrial Relations Journal*, 33: 20–35.

Hyman, R. (2006), Marxist thought and the analysis of work, in *Social Theory at Work*, edited by M. Korczynski, R. Hodson and P. Edwards, Oxford: Oxford University Press.

Hyman, R. (1989), *The Political Economy of Industrial Relations: Theory and Practice in a Cold Climate*, London: Macmillan.

Hyman, R. (1984), *Strikes*, London: Macmillan.

Hyman, R. (1975), *Industrial Relations, a Marxist introduction*, London: Macmillan.

Hyman, R. (1971), *Marxism and the Sociology of Trade Unionism*, London: Pluto Press.

Kelly, J. (1998), *Rethinking Industrial Relations: Mobilization, Collectivism and Long Waves*, London: LSE/Routledge.

Kelly, J. (1988), *Trade Unions and Socialist Politics*, London: Verso.

Kelly, J. and Badigannavar, V. (2005), Why are some union organizing campaigns more successful than others? *British Journal of Industrial Relations*, 43(3): 515–535.

James, D. (1990), *Resistencia e Integración: el Peronismo y la clase trabajadora argentina 1946–1976*, Buenos Aires: Editorial Sudamericana.

James, D. (1988), *Resistance and Integration: Peronism and the Argentinean Working Class*, Cambridge: Cambridge University Press.

Jitrik, N. (1987), Elements for an analysis of Argentine culture, in Peralta-Ramos, M. and Waisman, C.H. eds, *From Military Rule to Liberal Democracy in Argentina*, Westview Special Studies on Latin America and the Caribbean, Boulder, CO and London: Westview Press.

Jozami, E. (2000), *Ya nada será igual: la Argentina después del Menemismo*, Buenos Aires: Editorial Sudamericana.

Lane, T. and Roberts, K. (1971), *Strike at Pilkingtons*, London: Collins/Fontana.

Lebowitz, M. (2004), What keeps capitalism going? *Monthly Review*, 56: 2, available at http://www.monthlyreview.org/0604lebowitz.htm.

Lebowitz, M. (2003), *Beyond Capital. Marx's Political Economy of the Working Class*, London: Palgrave.

Lozano, C. and Basualdo, E. (2001), *A 25 años del golpe: la economía argentina luego de la dictadura*, Buenos Aires: IDEP.

Martuccelli, D. and Svampa, M. (1997), *La plaza vacía, las transformaciones del Peronismo*, Buenos Aires: Losada.

Marx, K. (1976), *Capital Volume 1*, London: Penguin.

Marx, K. (1852), The Eighteenth Brumaire of Louis Bonaparte, chapter 1, available at http://www.marxists.org/archive/marx/works/1852/18th-bru maire/ch01.htm.

Meardi, G. (2000), *Trade Unions Activists, East and West: Comparisons in Multinational Companies*, Gower: Aldershot.

Metochi, M. (2002), The influence of leadership and member attitudes in understanding the nature of union participation, *British Journal of Industrial Relations*, 40: 87–111.

Milkman, R (1997), *Farewell to the Factory: Autoworkers in the Late 20th Century*, Berkeley: University of California Press.

Moore, B. Jr (1978), *Injustice, the Social Bases of Obedience and Revolt*, New York: M.E. Sharp.

Munck, R., Falcón, R. and Gallittelli, B. (1987), *Argentina from Anarchism to Peronism: Workers, Unions and Politics, 1855–1985*, London: Zed Books.

Offe, C. and Wiesenthal, H. (1980), Two logics of collective action: theoretical notes on social class and organisational form, *Political Power and Social Theory*, 1: 67–115.

Palomino, H. (1985), El movimiento de democratización sindical, in Jenin, E. ed., Los nuevos Movimientos Sociales/2 Derechos Humanos Obreros, *Biblioteca Política Argentina*, Buenos Aires: CEAL.

Pion-Berlin, D. (1989), *The Ideology of State Terror: Economic Doctrine and Political Repression in Argentina and Perù*, Boulder, CO: Lynne Rienner Publishers.

Portelli, A. (1991), *The Death of Luigi Trastulli and Other Stories: Form and Meaning in Oral History*, Albany: State University of New York Press.

Pozzi, P. (1988), *Oposición obrera a la dictadura, 1976–1982*, Buenos Aires: Editorial Contrapunto.

Raimundo, M. (2000), Acerca de los orígenes del Peronismo revolucionario, in Camarero, H., Pozzi, P. and Schneider, A. eds, *De la revolución Libertadora al Menemismo, historia social y política Argentina*, Buenos Aires: Ediciones Imago Mundi.

Richards, D. (1995), Regional integration and class conflict: MERCOSUR and the Argentine labour movement appraisal, *Capital and Class*, 57: 55–82.

Rieser, V. (1997), *Lavorare a Melfi*, Rionero: Calice Editori.

Rosendahl, M. (1985), *Conflict and Compliance: Class Consciousness among Swedish Workers*, Stockholm Studies in Social Anthropology, 14, Stockholm: Stockholm University.

Roudil, H. (1993), La transición del sindicalismo argentino, in Moreno, O. ed., *Desafíos para el sindicalismo en la Argentina*, Buenos Aires: Fundación Ebert, Legasa.

Schvarzer, J. (1996), *La industria que supimos conseguir. Una historia político social de la industria argentina*, Buenos Aires: Planeta.

Silver, B. (2003), *Forces of Labor, Workers' Movements and Globalization since 1870*, Cambridge: Cambridge University Press.

Tedesco, L. (1999), *Democracy in Argentina. Hope and Disillusion*, London: Frank Cass.

Thompson, A. (1982), *Labour Struggles and Political Conflict. Argentina: the General Strike of 1975 and the Crisis of Peronism through an Historical Perspective*, Master thesis, Institute of Social Studies, The Hague.

Thompson, E.P. (1980), *The Making of the English Working Class*, London: Penguin.

Thwaites Rey, M. (1999), *Ajuste estructural y privatizaciones en la Argentina de los '90 (O como achicar el estado no es agrandar la nación)*, Doctoral thesis, University of Buenos Aires, Buenos Aires.

Torre, J.C. (1988), *La formación del sindicalismo Peronista*, Buenos Aires: Legasa.

Van der Linden, M. (2008), *Workers of the World: Essays Toward a Global Labour History*, Leiden: Brill.

Van der Velden, S., Dribbusch, H., Lyddon, D. Vandaele, K. (2007), *Strikes around the World, 1968–2005, Case Studies of 15 Countries*, Amsterdam: Aksant.

Waterman, P. and Wills, J. (2001), *Place, Space and the New Labour Internationalism*, Oxford: Blackwell.

Media and publications

Clarín, national newspaper.

La Voz del Interior, local newspaper.

Verdad Obrera, Trotskyist magazine.

Canal 10, Television Channel National University of Córdoba.

Cordobean Labour Movement Archive of the Biblioteca Popular de Bella Vista, Córdoba.

Index

169